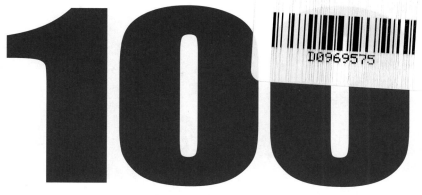

100

THINGS TO DO IN

TRAVERSE CITY

BEFORE YOU

DIE

100

THINGS TO DO IN

TRAVERSE CITY

BEFORE YOU

DIE

KIM SCHNEIDER

REEDY PRESS

Library of Congress Control Number: 2017957319

ISBN: 9781681060996

Design by Jill Halpin

Printed in the United States of America
18 19 20 21 22   5 4 3 2 1

Please note that websites, phone numbers, addresses, and company names are subject to change or cancellation. We did our best to relay the most accurate information available, but due to circumstances beyond our control, please do not hold us liable for misinformation. When exploring new destinations, please do your homework before you go.

DEDICATION

To Karl, my partner in stone skipping, sunset watching, Petoskey stone hunts . . . and life, and to Chris and Kayleigh. May your True North roots always guide you.

CONTENTS

• •

Music and Entertainment

• •

• •

Culture and History

Shopping and Fashion

• •

PREFACE

It wouldn't make for a very long book if I let you in on a secret. There's really only one thing you absolutely must do in or around Traverse City at some point in your life: look at the water . . . and that glimpse could come from a blanket at the beach, a downtown café while sipping a cocktail made from something cherry, or from atop a two-hundred-foot dune of sand that plummets straight down to a glimpse of a roaring Lake Michigan expanse you'll likely never forget.

In fact, you won't forget.

That view seeps into your soul and draws you back, and at some point in that stay or the one after or the one after that you'll get hungry, and then I'll want to tell you about these addictive croissants and sandwiches they make on this fresh pretzel bread in Fishtown and about this incredible young chef who transforms simple things into the best bite you can remember having.

I'll want to send you out onto the water in my favorite ways, like a tall ship cruise during which you really help raise those massive canvas sails and then eat ice cream or drink wine and sing along to sea shanties. Then you have my favorite events, and we have so many of them. I'll tell you not to miss the Big Wheel race or pit-spitting fun at the National Cherry Festival and how it's worth braving the Traverse City Film Festival line for free morning panel discussions with top directors and actors from around the world as they debate the biggest issues of our day. You also have to make a bonfire on the beach under the stars and maybe even snowshoe and bike. Then you need to tour a microbrewery or one of the scores of vineyards set on rolling hillsides along those waters with a color often compared to the Caribbean. The thing is: you really will want to do it all—and so I've tried to give you a head start with this list of one hundred ideas that somehow still just offers a sampling.

Traverse City has made so many lists of top places to visit in the past several years that we've pretty much stopped counting. But ask ten people to describe Traverse City in a word, and they seem to be talking about completely different places (one saying charming, another complex, one laid-back, another a place for adventure). That alone gives you a sense of all this big small town has to offer, says Traverse City Tourism president Trevor Tkach, a former head of the town's National Cherry Festival. What the area does, he says, is it "gently connects you to mother nature while subtly delivering sophistication."

Here, we think, you can live your best life—one that truly is a day at the beach and a whole lot more.

● ●

ACKNOWLEDGMENTS

Thanks to contributing writer Maura Brennan, founder of Sustainable TC, for lending her expertise as a local explorer and her writing talents for several items in the book, and to local winery expert Lorri Hathaway and her associates Chris O'Non and Erin Rose for their help in curating, research, and moral support. Credit for the cover image goes to the talented John Russell. Finally, thanks to area conservancies, community leaders, and friends at Traverse City Tourism for a vision that keeps the region's character and unparalleled natural resources intact even as opportunities and amenities grow.

FOOD AND DRINK

TOUR
WINE COUNTRY

If most everyone here knows the adage "People like to live where grapes like to grow," it's not due to envy of the winery château with cozy fireplaces, patios, and massive windows. It's because the tempering effect of Lake Michigan on climate extremes means that grapes often grow best on hillsides overlooking the water. That means the Traverse Wine Coast's forty-plus vineyards often serve up some of the region's best views as pairings for their estate-grown Riesling (the region's original signature grape), Chardonnay, Pinot Gris, Pinot Noir, and much more. Some, such as L. Mawby Vineyards, specialize only in sparkling wine, while others are known, too, for food pairings, live entertainment, vineyard snowshoe events, or creative help in upping your wine appreciation game.

For easy-to-follow wine trails and event listings:
wineriesofomp.com
lpwines.com
traversewinecoast.com

TIP
Check out guided fun options, which might mean a limo tour that lets someone else do the driving or perhaps the chance to traverse between wineries on snowshoes or even a fat-tire bike between the vines.

TRY SOME
OLD-FASHIONED CHERRY CHARCUTERIE

The nose-to-tail movement, or trend toward using the whole animal within the meal, has brought high-end butchery aplenty to the Traverse City area. But even visiting celebrity chefs get their grilling out fare at a small-town butcher shop in the Polish-settled community of Cedar. There, butcher and supportive dad Ray Pleva started experimenting the year his daughter Cindy was named National Cherry Queen. He replaced the fact in the meat with cherries, and his cherry pecan sausages and cherry-filled Plevalean burgers were such a surprise hit—and so good for you—that magazines such as *Food and Wine, Cooking Light* and *Men's Health* covered the story, forty-plus news crews flocked to Pleva's Meats, and "cherry burgers" started appearing on school lunch menus now in seventeen states. That said, these guilt-free indulgences are still best paired with a cookout at the cabin.

Pleva's Meat Market
8974 S Kasson St., Cedar
231-228-5000
plevasmeats.com

STARE DOWN
THE FISH IN YOUR DRINK

What started out as a joke has become a tourist draw to The Cove restaurant on Lake Michigan in Leland's historic Fishtown. First-time orderers of a Chubby Mary first gasp then quickly pull out the phone for a perfect Instagram-able moment when they see a smoked chub and its little fish face sticking out of the top of the glass next to a dill pickle, olive, and wedge of citrus. Then they "usually" realize that the smoky fish adds a perfect complement to the tomato, horseradish, citrus juices, and Worcestershire sauce. Even owner Rick Wanroy was surprised at its success, since he made it up on the spur of the moment when he was asked to name a signature cocktail and chopping up a fish inside a margarita proved to be an abysmal failure.

The Cove
111 River St., Leland
231-256-9834
plevasmeats.com

KEEP THE THEME GOING

Boone's Prime Time Pub

The "Massive Mary" comes with two actual burgers, onion rings, and more, all perched within your glass.

102 N St. Joseph St., Suttons Bay
231-271-6688
boonesprimetimepub.com

Pearl's New Orleans Kitchen

The crawfish in the glass pays homage to the restaurant's Cajun theme.

617 Ames St., Elk Rapids
231-264-0530
magnumhospitality.com

Short's Brewing Company

The Bloody (Mary) Beer is fermented with Roma tomatoes and spiced with dill, horseradish, peppercorns, and celery.

121 N Bridge St., Bellaire
231-498-2300
shortsbrewing.com

Northern Latitudes Distillery

Just add the Zing Zang. The locally distilled vodka comes infused with horseradish for easy beach cocktail making. Or, settle in for tastings and cocktails in house.

112 E Philip St., Lake Leelanau
231-256-2700
northernlatitudesdistillery.com

LET A (FUTURE) TOP CHEF
PAMPER YOU

There's no yelling from the kitchen Gordon Ramsay style, but fans of such shows as *Master Chef* get more pleasing benefits from meals prepared at Lobdell's by culinary students in training. The wall-to-ceiling glass windows overlook a private harbor, and Maritime Academy ships on Grand Traverse Bay offer the city's best dining view. The beautifully plated dishes are also a bargain at around ten dollars and up for the lunch main dish with soup or salad. It's also a bit of a secret. The restaurant is open only Tuesdays through Thursdays during class semesters, and the exclusivity gives you a fun chance to visit with students—and they range from those of traditional age to retired physicians and teachers—who rotate through cooking and serving positions.

Great Lakes Culinary Institute at Northwestern Michigan College
715 E Front St., Traverse City
231-995-3120

EAT
WITH A GHOST

There is that story about the exploding soufflé, but if you're not a nurse, you should be able to eat without interruption at Mission Table, where the ghost of a jilted lumber baron's wife named Genevive is said to haunt the elevator and be particularly nasty to nurses (the profession of her husband's mistress). Of all the local ghost stories, that of Genevive Stickney is the most persistent and even played upon; the chef has even teamed with winemakers and ghost whisperers on "Dine with Genevive" dinners. Many have headed to the bayside locale for wine and beer tasting or the three-course tasting dinner without incident, but do glance in the hallway mirror, where the image of a woman with hair in a tight bun has been spotted.

Mission Table Restaurant and Tasting Room
13512 Peninsula Dr., Traverse City
231-223-4222
missiontable.net

PLAY AN OLD-STYLE GAME
WITH A NEW-STYLE COCKTAIL

Michiganders learn euchre from an early age, and more than one friendship has perished when a partner's ace was inadvertently trumped. Not surprisingly, folks in Traverse City pull up a chair on Wednesdays in The Parlor for an old-fashioned card game played while sipping a new-style, pre-Prohibition cocktail. The onetime cherry cannery factory site now hosts tournaments every week from fall to spring. If you play your cards right, you can sample a signature craft cocktail, such as the Smoke Stack—local bourbon and a touch of maple syrup infused with cherry wood smoke. For a lighter option, regulars love the pineapple lemongrass mojito.

The Parlor
205 Lake Ave., Traverse City
231-753-3131, theparlortc.com

TIP

Just dive in. Euchre (yoo-ker) is a game with rules so confusing that it's best learned at the table, preferably from someone other than one's first partner. You'll learn about trumps and bauers and how jacks are sometimes the highest cards but sometimes not. But it's the game most quintessentially Michigan, and you have instant friends when you say, "Let's play euchre!"

TAKE A CRAFT COCKTAIL TOUR

Traverse City Whiskey Company
Try the American cherry version of
locally distilled spirits.

201 E 14th St., Traverse City
231-922-8292
tcwhiskey.com

Low Bar
Pre-Prohibition cocktail classics await in low lighting,
down an elevator with a doorman.

128 S Union St., Traverse City
231-944-5397
lowbartc.com

Olives and Wine
Seating options include a onetime bank vault, and
appetizers hail from the Mediterranean.

201 E Front St., Traverse City
231-943-2850
olivesandwine.com

PICNIC
WITH PURIS

Picnics are big here—beach picnics, cottage picnics, snacks-around-the-bonfire picnics—but when you want to move on from the grilled chicken/potato salad classics, head up the Leelanau Peninsula, where a trading post–style grocery of some form has served tiny Lake Leelanau (originally Provemont) since 1912. Inside deli containers in which elsewhere you might find potato salad, here you'll find puris and pakoras, fresh naan, and addictive chicken tikka masala.

N.J.'s Grocery mixes locally sourced wines, produce, and pies with the preferences of owners, who hail from India and brought family recipes along. Heat up what's prepackaged in the cooler, or call in an order from their India's Kitchen menu. Just be sure it includes samosas with a side of mint sauce; they're locally famous for a reason.

N.J.'s Grocery and India's Kitchen
115 W Philip St., Lake Leelanau
231-256-9195
njsgrocery.com

EAT (AND COOK)
FARMERS MARKET TO TABLE

Think little sister of Chez Panisse and you get The Cooks' House. Its chefs have even created community dinners jointly with and followed the playbook of Alice Waters, the pioneer of cuisine based on organic and locally grown produce. With just twenty-eight seats, it's also about as hard as at Chez Panisse to get a reservation, but that's because at this early-Victorian-era home-turned-restaurant, dinner might include a savory Hubbard squash crème brûlée topped with a bhel puri appetizer that combines styles of chef partners Eric Patterson and Jennifer Blakeslee. One way to get in—and into the kitchen—is to sign up for a cooking class that starts at the farmers market and, notes Patterson, "gives people an opportunity to see the beginning and end of a dish and how we think as chefs."

The Cooks' House
115 Wellington St., Traverse City
231-946-8700
cookshousetc.com

TIP
In peak season, tables fill about three weeks in advance, so get reservations as you're planning your visit, or make your spur-of-the-moment trips midweek in late fall or winter.

DIP INTO CHOCOLATE
DONE THE BETTER WAY

If there's one can't-miss destination for culinary food tours and the average vacationer alike, it's Grocer's Daughter Chocolate. The quirky chartreuse exterior along M-22 just outside Empire gives nod to the fun and warm welcome you'll find inside but not necessarily the other things that set this artisan chocolate shop apart. There's such a close connection to growers in such countries as Ecuador that owners Jody and DC Hayden travel annually to buy chocolate from farmers, take it to processing plants for fermentation and roasting, and then, back in Empire, marry it with local flavors like honey, whiskey, or garden herbs. On a cool day, make your reward their rich hot chocolate topped with whipped cream from Shetler's dairy cream sweetened with maple syrup, topped with a chocolate-dipped turkish fig filled with whiskey ganache, and served in a locally made Skipping Stone Pottery mug.

Grocer's Daughter Chocolate
12020 S Leelanau Hwy. (M-22), Empire
231-326-3030
grocersdaughter.com

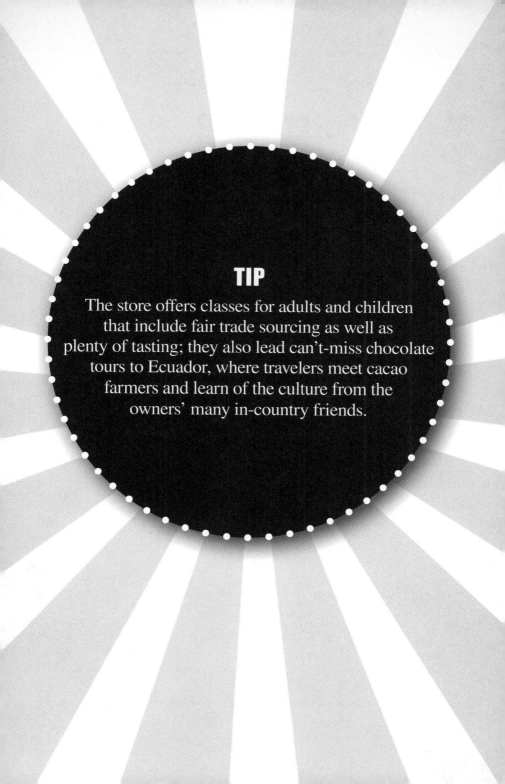

TIP

The store offers classes for adults and children that include fair trade sourcing as well as plenty of tasting; they also lead can't-miss chocolate tours to Ecuador, where travelers meet cacao farmers and learn of the culture from the owners' many in-country friends.

LINGER
OVER BRUNCH

If the soft morning light and corner model of the Eiffel Tower don't have you saying "c'est magnifique," the sauces, crepes, and light-as-air beignets at Patisserie Amie will. Try the Saumon au Four (salmon fillet, poached eggs, caviar, and hollandaise) or the blueberry blintz with its warm cheese dripping from sweet blueberry-filled pastry. Expect long weekend waits, but that just means time to ponder the art-worthy pastry case. Plated brunches are served, too, at The Franklin, set apart by its cuisine, rooftop patio views, and creative cocktails, and The Towne Plaza, notable for creative uses of pork, such as Tasso ham in your Benedict. Those who like variety will love the traditional (in variety, though not offerings) brunches at Aerie, with its tower bay view, and Apache Trout Grill, set along the bay.

Patisserie Amie
237 Lake Ave., #200, Traverse City
231-922-9645
patisserieamietc.com

Aerie
100 Grand Traverse Village Blvd., Acme
231-534-6800
grandtraverseresort.com

The Franklin
160 E Front St., Traverse City
231-943-2727

Apache Trout Grill
13671 S West Bay Shore Dr., Traverse City
231-947-7079
apachetroutgrill.com

The Towne Plaza
203 Cass St., Traverse City
231-929-0900
thetowneplaza.com

LET
THE FOOD TRUCKS LEAD

Gary and Allison Jonas are experts at creating environments that make people want to celebrate. In Brooklyn, they opened a combination flower shop and bar, while in Traverse City, they formed Little Fleet, transforming a former parking lot into an outdoor food truck collective, indoor bar, and family-friendly community gathering place.

One weekend a marching band might be playing a fight song as kickoff for a collegiate football viewing party inside. On another food truck, favorites may be enjoyed while sitting around a fire pit, playing bingo, shopping from local artists, dancing, or eating soup at a community fund-raiser. Any day you can simply picnic with a made-to-order food truck meal of sushi, Korean beef tacos, or Cooks' House curry, eaten inside or out with a fresh-squeezed margarita or two.

Little Fleet
448 E Front St., Traverse City
thelittlefleet.com

EAT YOUR ICE CREAM
"COW TO CONE"

There's a small but obvious downside to sampling your Cherries Moobilee blend of Traverse City cherries, chocolate fudge, and brownie chunks while gazing over a pastoral scene that includes the cows that provided the cream—depending, of course, on the direction of the wind. But combining one spouse's dairy farming background with the other's background in education has proven serendipitous to the owners of Moomer's ice cream shop in Traverse City. The farm-based restaurant was an insider hit already when *Good Morning America* named theirs the best ice cream in America; likely, few other spots let you pair a tasting of up to 160 flavors (twenty served at any given time) with a six-dollar wagon ride to the dairy farm for milk tasting and a barn and creamery tour.

Moomer's
7263 N Long Lake Rd., Traverse City
231-941-4122
moomers.com

PICK UP DINNER
IN THE WOODS

People in Michigan's North are friendly enough to share almost anything—probably even the souvenir sweatshirt off their backs. Just don't even think of asking where they find their morel mushrooms. The northern delicacy of the woods is the most prized food of spring and about as expensive if you want to pick them up in a grocery store as a truffle might set you back in France. Eating them, though, is best done in a very unfussy way—dredged in flour, fried in butter—and there are many safe paths to the find. The Boyne Morel Mushroom festival offers a guided hunt and the Taste of Morel samplings prepared by chefs, as does a Black Star Farms harvest dinner. Mesick's Mushroom Festival offers a six-dollar kit with a treasure map to good hunting spots.

Black Star Farms
10844 E Revold Rd., Suttons Bay
231-944-1270, blackstarfarms.com

Boyne City Morel Festival, bcmorelfestival.com

Mesick Mushroom Festival, mesick-mushroomfest.org

TIP

"False morels" can be poisonous, so to know if you've found an edible one, cut the mushroom in half from the tip of the cap to the bottom of the stem. Safe ones are hollow through the entire inside length of the mushroom.

KISS A MOOSE,
EAT A BURGER

You're not supposed to think too closely about such things as how many other people have kissed Randolph the (stuffed) moose (head) at Sleder's Family Tavern. It's just what you do. You kiss the moose. Someone rings a bell. Everyone in the restaurant cheers, just as they might have done in 1882 when it opened as a social club for Bohemian woodworkers. Sleder's is the oldest continually operating restaurant in Michigan, and that its popularity hasn't waned is due to the cool carved bar, stuffed animal heads, frequent live music, and tasty salads and burgers—some featuring meat sourced from a local buffalo herd. It's also an anchor in Slabtown, named for the way homes were built from pieces of scrap wood salvaged from mills but today noted for bakeries, ice cream shops, and uncrowded beaches.

Sleder's Family Tavern
717 Randolph St., Traverse City
231-947-9213
sleders.com

ORDER "WATER"
WITH YOUR MEAL

"Where can we eat on the water?" It's the most common restaurant question asked in Northern Michigan, and no wonder. Grand Traverse Bay and its often Caribbean-style blues make a perfect pairing with any dining experience, and there's really nothing more romantic than dining over a Lake Michigan sunset, at least if you can resist gazing into the camera instead of your dining partner's eyes. Settle for a water view from a distant rooftop and you have even more options, but on-water dining means such favorites as special-occasion Blu in Glen Arbor, where you want to time reservations to catch a setting sun out the wall of windows or more casual dining on such items as fried perch-in-a-cone at Knot Just a Bar on gorgeous Omena Bay. Everything pairs well with the bay view at West End Tavern in Traverse City.

Blu
5705 S Lake St., Glen Arbor
231-334-2530, glenarborblu.com

Knot Just a Bar
5019 N West Bay Shore Dr., Omena
231-386-7393, knotjustabar.com

West End Tavern
12719 S West Bay Shore Dr., Traverse City
231-943-2922, westendtaverntc.com

SIP
AMID CELEBS

Name-dropping comes easily at Traverse City area wineries, and we're not talking your ask for another pour of Pino Noir or unoaked Chardonnay. Many local vintners are true wine world celebrities for their many awards and innovations. But that also may be actress Amy Smart on that old tractor amid the vines. She's a part owner of popular Bonobo Winery on the Old Mission Peninsula. Winery neighbors include Mari Vineyards, at which owners Marty and Alex Lagina might be spotted when not treasure hunting on History Channel's *The Curse of Oak Island*. These newer wineries take some pressure off Madonna's dad, Tony Ciccone, owner of one of the area's original wineries on the Leelanau Peninsula and where her sister and brother make the wine and tend the vineyards. Just don't think celebrity means snobby; all three offer cozy fireplace corners and patios with views that encourage lingering.

Bonobo Winery
12011 Center Rd., Traverse City
231-282-9463, bonobowinery.com

Mari Vineyards
8175 Center Rd., Traverse City
231-938-6116, marivineyards.com

Ciccone Vineyard & Winery
10343 E Hilltop Rd., Suttons Bay
231-271-5553, cicconevineyard.com

TIP

Ask about special guided tours or tastings, offered at most area wineries and sometimes conducted by the winemakers themselves. At Mari, tours include education about their unusual wine making process and a private tasting of wines still aging in barrels. At Bonobo, the VIP tour (minimum six people) gives you reserved seating, a private server and personalized tour of the facility and vineyards.

BREW UNTO OTHERS
AT WORKSHOP BREWING

"Stranger Brew" could refer to such beer names as the Cold Chisel and Ten Pound Sledge or Capitalist Pig (pulled pork) at Workshop Brewing Company, but at this casual gathering spot, owners focus on creating community with various initiatives, such as "Brew Unto Others," through which you score a discount when you pay it forward with a drink for a friend who couldn't make it that day and whose name goes on a board indicating a drink is waiting. Stranger Brew takes it beyond, letting you leave a freebie for whomever you pen on a note: a Navy Seal, a parent with an autistic child, even someone in a kilt. It's a twist on many other reasons to pop in—maybe free concerts by the area's best bands, storytelling sessions, even church.

Workshop Brewing Company
221 Garland St., Traverse City
231-421-8977
traversecityworkshop.com

NO SOUP FOR YOU
EXCEPT ON WEDNESDAYS

Known as the place to go for a good greasy breakfast, an after-ski warmup, or the last call after a day of fun, Art's Tavern in downtown Glen Arbor is also renowned for the Chicken Jalapeño Soup, inexplicably only available on Wednesday. Visitors and locals plan their week around the weekly sampling of creamy soup with just the right amount of kick.

Don't let the jalapeño inclusion scare you. Many other non-jalapeño lovers have been converted as they try their first taste on the outdoor patio or in the beer garden or inside the bar filled with friendly locals. And stick around. Look closely and you'll see the square in the middle of the bar. Come evening, the staff pushes tables to the side and lifts out the pool table hidden beneath.

Art's Tavern
6487 W Western Ave., Glen Arbor
231-334-3754
artsglenarbor.com

TIP
Bring cash. Art's Tavern is one of the few businesses left that don't take plastic.

STAY
FOR SUNDAY SUPPER

When restaurants quiet slightly but harvest bounty is at its peak, some local chefs offer family-style Sunday suppers. At The Tribune Ice Cream and Eatery, named for the newspapers once produced in the building near Northport's waterfront and carrying on the tradition with menus that look like a paper, that means five-course farm-to-table meals served among no more than twenty lucky guests. Themes might be the Basque region of Spain or Thai or Eastern European cuisine, but the common thread is that the food is always fresh and locally sourced.

During warmer weather, breakfast and lunch guests (dinners are only offered on Sunday) can sit on the roomy rear deck; and waits are easy. A staff member will take your number so you can stroll local gift shops and galleries.

The Tribune Ice Cream and Eatery
110 E Nagonaba St., Northport
231-386-1055
northporttribune.com

TIP
Plan your vacation around the Tribune. On the upper floor of the restaurant is a vacation rental that sleeps up to six.

CELEBRATE ARTISANS
AT YOUR TABLE

"A farmer married a baker." That's both the beginning of a great story and a great restaurant/farm/bakery empire of sorts. Visit their bakery, restaurant or farmers market booth and you'll see why each year they hand-shape (just for local sale) some seventy thousand flaky 9 Bean Row croissants stuffed with almond paste, chocolate, or spinach and feta. Thank Jen Welty's training with Belgian bakers, a modified Julia Childs recipe, and the same passion for her craft that husband Nic brings to the growing of most of what's served in their 9 Bean Rows restaurant in Suttons Bay. Or take home an artisan bread loaf and pair with the work of more local artisans of cheese. Leelanau Cheese's Ann and John Hoyt don't bring Swiss cows down from the mountain anymore, but they similarly craft their internationally prize-winning raclette.

Leelanau Cheese Company
3324 S West Bay Shore Dr., Suttons Bay
231-271-2600
leelanaucheese.com

9 Bean Rows
303 N St. Joseph St., Suttons Bay
231-271-1175
9beanrows.com

MUNCH
A CENTURIES-OLD APPLE (TYPE)

John Kilcherman grew up playing baseball in his dad's Northport orchard on Sunday afternoons, running to the Wealthy tree for first base, the Snow Apple for second, and so on. When he married Phyllis, they decided to plant some nostalgic varieties, and they kept planting those named Pippin and Maiden's Blush and Spitzelberg and Summer Rambo—that one the favorite of another John, Johnny Appleseed. At the seasonally operated store, find almost enough options for an apple a day a year without repeating yourself and even more antique pop bottles—the some ten thousand lining the walls are enough to qualify for a Guinness record. If you can't match your name to a bottle, you'll easily match an apple to a taste preference or the memory of the type that held your childhood tire swing.

Kilcherman's Christmas Cove Farm
11573 N Kilcherman Rd., Northport
231-386-5637
christmascovefarm.com

TIP

Don't leave without a pint or more of the most complex cider you're likely to taste—one blended from whatever apples are available at the time—and know that the mix gets darker and richer the longer the season goes on.

SEE
WHAT THE BUZZ IS ABOUT

When it's 5:00 p.m. in downtown Traverse City, locals head for Red Ginger to meet up with friends and melt off the stress of the day with a craft cocktail. The upscale atmosphere and unique Asian fusion food and drinks keep the bar crowded with those in the know choosing the signature Red Dragon martini and pairing that with a selection from the specially priced happy hour menu of sushi, lettuce wraps, and Vietnamese spring rolls. For that special meal out, reserve ahead of time for a table at tiny Alliance in the up-and-coming Warehouse District. The ambience is loud, the kitchen open, the taste combinations sensational. Let your knowing waiter guide selections served as sharing portions. Even humble beets make for a most memorable bite the way they're prepared and sauced.

Red Ginger
237 E Front St., Traverse City
231-944-1733
eatatginger.com

Alliance
144 Hall St., #107, Traverse City
231-642-5545
foodforalliance.com

HIP HAPPY HOURS

Bistro Foufou

The gourmet French appetizers make the happy hour at Bistro Foufou an international experience.

bistrofoufou.com

Firefly

With $3 wines and $2 drinks, Firefly, on the Boardman River, is the best bang in town for your happy hour buck.

tcfirefly.com

Sorellina

It is always happy hour in the lounge at Sorellina Italian restaurant (think peach bellini and thin crust pizza).

sorrelinatc.com

PARTAKE
IN A FISH BOIL

New Orleans has the po-boy, New England the clambake, and Traverse City the fish boil. There are mixed opinions on how good fish tastes when simply boiled with potatoes and onions and served slathered with butter (and followed by pie), but the ritual is undeniably delicious when paired with a story about Great Lakes fishing and a dramatic flame during boil-over as done every summer and autumn Friday at Black Star Farms. The region grew up on its fishing heritage, and if you don't take yours boiled (or fried or baked) at any local restaurant, buy fresh from Native American fishermen at the Duhamel Marina in Peshawbestown or the Carlson family, where smoked fish and dip are hot sellers at their Fishtown shop, and you may watch them hauling in their catch.

Black Star Farms
10844 E Revold Rd., Suttons Bay
blackstarfarms.com
231-944-1270

Carlson's Fish
205 River St., Leland
231-256-9801
carlsonsfish.com

SLURP VINEGAR
[ON PURPOSE]

Hear the concept and many are skeptical—take samples of oil, pour into tiny paper cup, and slurp. Do the same with vinegars, then mix and match for your bread dipping, grill meat basting, salad topping, and more. Fustini's (named after the silver jugs holding the goodies), is the brainchild of a former marketer at 3M, the Minnesota conglomerate known for innovation, and it found a fast following among people who basically like to play amateur scientist with their food, kind of grade-school lunchroom style but with way fancier ingredients. Does Sicilian lemon vinegar work with Barbary Coast oil? Is the Piedmont honey oil tastier with oil tinged with fig—or cayenne crush? Wisely, trained mixologists help lead the experimenting, and an on-site chef offers popular cooking classes at the in-store teaching kitchen.

Fustini's Oils and Vinegars
141 E Front St., Traverse City
fustinis.com

EAT PIE

It's as simple as this. You can't go to the country's cherry capital and not eat pie. Cherry pie. You're welcome, too, to the cherry chicken salads, the cherry salsas, cherry whiskies, cherries covered with chocolate, and the cherry wine, but at the end of the meal, in between, or even for breakfast, the must-eat is at least one slice or whole pie (crumble or regular crust, with the addition of other berries, or not) from the Grand Traverse Pie Company. If it's not the best cherry pie in the world, it's at least a close runner-up in a place with the best cherries. As a bonus, this homegrown company dedicates profits from its community shop (of its two Front Street shops, the one near the State Theatre) to child abuse prevention. The signature heart at the center of its pies says it all.

Grand Traverse Pie Company
525 W Front St., Traverse City
231-922-7437
gtpie.com

The Cherry Connection
12414 Center Rd. (M-37), Traverse City
231-223-7130
facebook.com/Cherry-Connection-of-Edmondson-Or-
chards-290550187718099/

The Cherry Hut
211 N Michigan Ave., Beulah
231-882-2431
cherryhut.com

● ●

TIP

For the full experience, pick your own red, ripe cherries straight from the tree at The Cherry Connection. Still hungry? Travel-worthy pie awaits at Beulah's fun The Cherry Hut, in business for nearly a century and easy to find by the smiling "Cherry Jerry" face on its sign.

CATCH
SOME COFFEE CULTURE

If a city's coffee shops are key to understanding its culture, you might call Traverse City's eclectic. Brew, on Front Street, is where you'll catch a mix of the hipster crowd, professionals holding meetings or catching up on work assignments, and anyone who has discovered the one-dollar self-serve coffee option. BLK Market is a favorite for its sweet and savory baked goods, passion for craft, and bay windows open barn-door style to distant peeks of the bay. Higher Grounds Coffee inspires loyalty for its dedication not just to fair trade coffee but also to changing the lives of farmers and villagers in their coffee-growing regions—and also for the way a latte might start with both the vanilla bean and locally sourced Shelter Farms milk.

Brew
108 E Front St., Traverse City
231-946-2739
brewtc.com

BLK Market
144 Hall St., Traverse City
231-714-5038
blkmrkt.coffee

Higher Grounds Coffee
806 Red Dr., Traverse City
231-922-9009
highergroundstrading.com

TIP

Sign up for one of Higher Grounds' regular coffee cupping classes, a learning experience not unlike a guided wine tasting.

MUSIC AND ENTERTAINMENT

TAKE
A 45TH PARALLEL SELFIE

A conservation club once created a 140-mile path across Michigan they called the Polar-Equator Trail, with the goal of rivaling the Oregon or Appalachian Trails, but people kept stealing the signs and getting lost. Today, you'll best capture your unique spot in the world—halfway between the equator and north pole (three thousand miles from each)—with a photo. Several of the twenty-nine signs denoting this spot in the world across the United States are in Michigan's north, though the imaginary line also crosses the world's most famous wine regions, including Bordeaux, the location of the ancient silk trade, and the deserts of Mongolia. You'll find one photo opp on M-31 near Elk Rapids, another by the lighthouse on the Old Mission Peninsula, and another on M-22 north of Suttons Bay.

TIP
Take a dip too. An ancient legend holds that anyone who bathes in waters crossed by the 45th parallel will be cured of ailments. At the very least, wade your cares away at the 45th Parallel beach park, marked by a boulder, north of Suttons Bay.

DRIVE UP
TO THE MOVIE

Among the things that should never go extinct and fortuitously haven't yet in Northern Michigan is the drive-in. Twilight lingers in Traverse City come peak summer, so we slip in a nap to fit in the double feature that may not begin until almost 10 p.m. But at the Cherry Bowl, the fun starts on the putt-putt golf course, with the popcorn (with real butter), the pre-movie vintage cartoons, and time to settle into the back of a truck with pillows and blankets (slippers optional).

All movies here are guaranteed to be G, PG, or PG-13, meaning it's always family friendly. While the sound quality of the speakers may take you too far back, you can also stream sound through your car speakers.

Cherry Bowl Drive-In
9812 Honor Hwy., Honor
231-325-3413
cherrybowldrivein.com

BROWSE ART
WITH YOUR MUSIC

Come winter the music is the squeaky swish of your snowshoes as you wander otherwise silent woods amid forty-seven art installations that tell the story of Michigan in particularly inventive ways on the 1.6 miles of trails on the grounds of the Crystal Mountain ski resort in Thompsonville. Haunting silhouettes represent the loggers who once clear-cut the state's dense forests. A two-headed deer offers a tribute to wildlife, and then there are outlines that capture Ernest Hemingway, a longtime vacationer in the state, at various stages of his life, or portray a character in one his book.

Founder and artist David Barr envisioned the nonprofit as a place to connect "man to nature and nature to man," and those connections are heightened in summer when a concert series brings Celtic, folk, indie rock, and other tunes wafting through.

Michigan Legacy Art Park and Summer Sounds Concert Series
7300 Mountainside Dr., Thompsonville
231-378-4963
michlegacyartpark.org/events/summer-sounds

HIT A FAMILY-FRIENDLY CONCERT
IN A HOPS LOT (OR TRAIN DEPOT)

Some of the area's best bands and solo singers regularly perform free concerts on cozy outdoor patios at microbreweries and wineries—some of which boast the region's best views.

Most are also family friendly. At the Hop Lot microbrewery and restaurant, your privacy fence is a curtain of hops, your warmth-provider a couple of roaring fires, and the band likely to join you at a communal picnic table or in making s'mores from the one dollar kits offered at the bar. Sandboxes surround the tables by the rails at The Filling Station Microbrewery, a restored train depot, where you'll hear some of the area's most popular bands with your wood-fired pizzas. Lovers of great wine and views will love Rove Estate, situated on Leelanau County's highest point and where children dance to live Celtic patio tunes.

Hop Lot Brewing Company
658 S West Bay Shore Dr., Suttons Bay
231-866-4445, hoplotbrewing.com

The Filling Station Microbrewery
642 Railroad Pl., Traverse City
231-946-8168, thefillingstationmicrobrewery.com

Rove Estate
7007 E Traverse Hwy., Traverse City
231-421-7001, roveestate.com

FETE THE ASPARAGUS

It might be a sign of spring fever that one of spring's first festivals has visitors dressing up in headpieces decked with a stalk of asparagus, painting faces (and wine and beer) green, and even writing poetry about a vegetable in the annual "Ode to Asparagus" competition.

It's easy and never more fun being green than in Empire, late May, when stalks are at their ripest and Northern Michiganders fete the humble vegetable in a party of games, parades, food, dancing, and drinking. There's even spear beer from Traverse City's Right Brain Brewery and sometimes green (asparagus, not Irish) wine as well. There's also a wildly popular and even more creative poetry contest as well as food. Asparagus is served up on focaccia and pizza or in risotto, scones, bratwurst, chocolate, and in ever-surprising ways during the popular annual cookoff.

Empire Asparagus Festival
empirechamber.com

CATCH A CONCERT
AT INTERLOCHEN CENTER
FOR THE ARTS

A summer concert at Interlochen's open-air Kresge Auditorium amphitheater just minutes outside Traverse City is as much a social event as it is a chance to catch some of the nation's most popular classic rock bands, folk musicians, or classical groups. People tailgate in the parking lot or buy treats in the center of a campus populated by some of the nation's most talented students in music, theater, visual arts, creative writing, film, and dance. But while creative energy—and music—is always wafting through the tall campus pines, it's hard to beat seeing ZZ Top or Diana Ross on a stage with a lake as a backdrop. Other year-round offerings might include The Wailin' Jennys, David Sedaris, *The Nutcracker*, or the Juilliard String Quartet.

Interlochen Center for the Arts
4000 M-137, Interlochen
231-276-7200
interlochen.org

SAIL, THE FUN WAY

By day you'll hula hoop on the catamaran deck to Disney tunes and a donut snack; by night those hula hoops may be glowing, and you'll groove next to fire poi dancers while enjoying local bands and champagne. The forty-seven-foot *Nauti-Cat* is the largest commercial sailing catamaran on the Great Lakes. Take the champagne sunset cruise (forty dollars) and relax on netted beds poised over the water, and bring your own picnic, such as the Gobbler, a local favorite from Mary's Kitchen Port. Weekend cruises offers dancing into the midnight hours and the popular "shot-ski" (up to forty dollars). The kids cruise (fiteen dollars a person) offers the region's best on-the-water deal and tame but memorable fun, such as blowing bubbles and helping raise and lower sails.

Nauti-Cat Cruises
615 E Front St., Traverse City
231-464-6080
nauti-cat.com

GO
TO THE NORTHWESTERN MICHIGAN FAIR

With more than fifty thousand acres of land under cultivation, Grand Traverse County is at its heart a farming community, and that, lucky visitor, means an annual old-timey fair complete with cornmeal-battered deep-fried hot dogs on a stick. Since 1908 the Northwestern Michigan Fair has celebrated the agriculture and "domestic science" of the community. Check out the prized livestock of 4-H kids, maybe even pet one, watch the horse show, and bid on a quilt in the ladies' raffle.

At dusk, throw back and take in a rodeo, a truck pull, or even a demolition derby. Of course, there are also carnival rides for the kiddos, but let's be frank. You're there for the food; here, there's no judging when you order a puff pastry dripping with butter and cinnamon that is bigger than your head.

Northwestern Michigan Fair
3606 Blair Town Hall Rd., Traverse City
231-943-4150
northwesternmichiganfair.net

CATCH A FLICK
IN A CLASSIC DOWNTOWN THEATER

Date night in Traverse City and many surrounding towns is still centered around catching a flick at an old-style cinema, but there's also a lot of new style in the State Theatre and the waterfront Bijou by the Bay, Traverse City's newly remodeled movie houses, both operated entirely by volunteers.

Renovation details went as far as having a car manufacturer create extra-roomy seats for the State and an on-ceiling replica of the star locations of Traverse City's night sky. Nearly a century old, the State has now made such lists as the "Ten Best Movie Theaters in the World" and also prompted the opening of many nearby restaurants and cocktail bars. Best, though, is the affordability and fun; every weekend and some weekdays bring quarter matinees. Worth the trip alone is the pre-holiday lineup of classic Christmas flicks that just may include a visit from a live reindeer.

State Theatre and Bijou by the Bay
stateandbijou.org

SAY "LIVE...
IT'S FRIDAY NIGHT"

After the Cherry Festival crowds go home, locals (and lucky visitors) flock to downtown Traverse City on August Fridays when Front Street gets blocked off for an old-fashioned community party. Street vendors line the sidewalks, and live music fills the air. Grab a gyro from the U&I Lounge and stroll through the crowds, perusing the tables set up by local nonprofits, many with hands-on activities for children. Jugglers, magicians, balloon twisters, caricature artists, and face painters entertain along the route. Join in or people-watch from an outdoor café. Either way don't forget to get some warm gourmet kettle corn from Pop-Kie's on your way home.

Friday Night Live
100 and 200 blocks of Front St., Traverse City
downtowntc.com/event/friday-night-live

DANCE BAREFOOT
IN THE GRASS

Kick off your shoes and kick up your heels. When the days get long and the breeze off the bay turns warm, Northern Michigan's summer concert scene brings barefoot toe tappin'. The Manitou Music Festival brings folk, jazz, and blues to various idyllic outdoor locations in Leelanau County (think lying on a blanket at the foot of a dune). On Thursday evenings, the free Concerts on the Lawn at the Grand Traverse Pavilions is the perfect spot for a family picnic. The Fountain Point Resort concert series offers local musical favorites on the lawn of a historic inn. Pack your cooler with hors d'oeuvres, throw in your favorite bottle of vino, and head for the hills (or the dune or the meadow).

Glen Arbor Art Association
Manitou Music Festival
6031 S Lake St., Glen Arbor
231-334-6112
manitoumusicfestival.com

Grand Traverse Pavilions
1000 Pavilions Clr., Traverse City
231-932-3000
gtpavilions.org

Fountain Point Music
990 S Lake Leelanau Dr., Lake Leelanau
231-256-9800
fountainpointmusic.com

HEAR THE SUNSET
THROUGH JAZZ

Estate-grown wine, live music, and views of surrounding vineyards, islands, and bays make for the ultimate summer outing combo. A growing number of wineries offer live music from patios, but Chateau Chantal maybe launched it all with its ongoing Jazz at Sunset, featuring the Jeff Haas Trio.

The winery is nestled on an Old Mission Peninsula hilltop, with sweeping views of East and West Grand Traverse Bay, and Haas, the pianist and frontman, is a Detroit native whose father hosted a classical music program for decades on public radio. He has become both a popular performer and an ambassador for music and its potential to bridge racial and social divides. Often joined by saxophonist Laurie Sears, the trio offers a varied repertoire, ranging from masters, such as Duke Ellington and John Coltrane, to modern composers, including Haas himself.

Chateau Chantal
15900 Rue de Vin, Traverse City
231-223-4110
chateauchantal.com

PICNIC
AT THE OPERA HOUSE

In a region where (elevated) potlucks remain a trendy way to entertain, it's maybe not a big surprise that we put a beachy spin even on such cultural events as "Picnic at the Opera." Event-goers are invited to pull out their wicker basket or brown bag (no judging) as they act as live audience for an old-fashioned variety show. The circa-1892 City Opera House was the first building in Traverse City to have electric lights. Now fully restored, even to the cherubs on the ceiling, it offers a grand backdrop to Picnic at the Opera and to the national performing arts series also held here. Check the schedule to see a Grammy Award-winning band or an off-Broadway show or to hear authors sharing stories behind their work at the National Writers Series, which regularly brings a celebrated global lineup of writers to town.

City Opera House
106 E Front St., Traverse City
231-941-8082
cityoperahouse.org

DO EXPERIMENTS
BY SHIP

The nonprofit Inland Seas Education Association has successfully bet that the best way to help protect the Great Lakes and the 20 percent of the world's freshwater that it holds is by letting people get their hands wet. On a pirate ship.

Well, the ship is actually a seventy-seven-foot traditionally rigged schooner, but its dark sails when spotted on the bay bring to mind a swarthy Johnny Depp. There may also be some pirate-style singing on board as visitors (some trips are for students; others are for tourists and families) dip for water samples and study them under onboard microscopes. The goal is to protect the lakes by conducting research and igniting curiosity. You can also sign up to run a remotely activated vehicle on a lake bottom or build an old-fashioned sailing vessel.

Inland Seas Education Association
100 Dame St., Suttons Bay
231-271-3077
schoolship.org

CATCH A WHOLE LOTTA FILMS
AT THE TRAVERSE CITY FILM FESTIVAL

Even many locals plan their vacation time around the Traverse City Film Festival, a multiday series of documentaries, first-run motion pictures, foreign films, and other "just great movies." Filmmaker and now local Michael Moore is in charge of the lineup, shown at several venues around town. There's an opening night street party with a bit of Hollywood glitz and also free filmmaker panels, film classes, and outdoor family movies by the bay. One highlight is having many actors and directors hold Q&A sessions at their films; their presence is noted in the movie schedule. Regular shuttles between venues take care of the logistics.

traversecityfilmfest.org

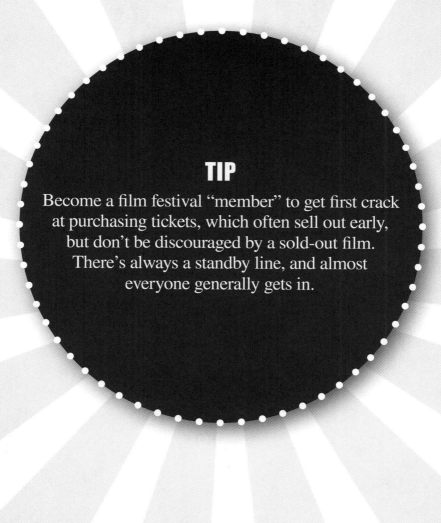

TIP

Become a film festival "member" to get first crack
at purchasing tickets, which often sell out early,
but don't be discouraged by a sold-out film.
There's always a standby line, and almost
everyone generally gets in.

PUT A CHERRY
ON TOP

It's loud, downtown gets crazy, and you may find yourself grousing about finding a place to park, but you will likely also find yourself smiling through the eight-day National Cherry Festival, often named in *USA Today*'s list of the country's top ten, as you help to usher in the festival's second century of celebrating all things cherry. The early-July start generally coincides with harvest in a region that produces more than 650 million pounds of tart and sweet cherries each year. Prepare to eat your share in free pie-eating contests and pit-spitting competitions, drink them in wine, and celebrate them in runs and art shows and Navy Blue Angels air shows, but also take tours exploring the region's rich agricultural traditions.

National Cherry Festival
cherryfestival.org

"WINE" DOWN
AT A WINERY B&B

It's just plain handy to just walk down a hall to your room after a day of wine tasting, but there's much more to recommend the charm and amenities of Traverse City's three winery bed-and-breakfast options, which are unique in the state. At Chateau Chantal, you score a Tuscan-style hilltop view of classic red barns and distant islands, and add-on room service options are available, ranging from fondue to mulled wine with cheese plate and fresh baguette. Hard to beat, though, is the chance to taste wine with other guests after the tasting room is closed, then move on to board games by the real wood fire. At Chateau Grand Traverse, your view is also vineyards and bay, with an entire home yours for the roaming. And at the Inn at Black Star Farms, dinner's across the street at their on-site restaurant, but you may not even need it after the private wine and appetizers by their fireplace.

traversewinecoast.com

SPORTS AND RECREATION

HIKE
TO A COLOR TOUR VISTA

Named for the high banks that allowed lumbermen to roll trees into the Manistee River destined for sawmills downstream, the Highbanks Rollaway Trail (aka the High Rollaways) is a local favorite. In fact, you may need a local to help you find the trailhead (it's at the end of an unnamed road outside the tiny town of Buckley). Those who persevere will be rewarded by a breathtaking view at the scenic overlook, where miles and miles of dense hardwood forest can be seen from a bird's-eye view, two hundred feet above the Manistee River Valley. Follow the nearby trail that winds along the bluffs high above the meandering river. Locals return every fall when the lush forest view is set on fire by autumn's bright oranges, yellows, and reds.

Highbanks Rollaway Trail, Buckley
866-445-3628 (North Country Trail Association)
northcountrytrail.org/gtr/directions/

GO ON A TREASURE HUNT
FOR FREEBIES

Getting free stuff is fun anyway, but a genius marketing staff made it even better by sending anyone who books a two-night stay in the county on a treasure hunt to the region's coolest (and tastiest) attractions. Book the Benzie Treasure Trove and you get to eat pie, float the Betsie River, tour a lighthouse, snack on breadsticks, bike a trail, sip a root beer float, munch on movie popcorn, and more—all free, for at least one member of the group. Fit them all in and you've saved up to three hundred dollars (more than many lodging options will cost you), but you'll have fun trying even if you barely make it past the free Crescent Bakery donut that had a cameo in locally filmed *Youth in Revolt*.

Benzie County Visitors Bureau
826 Michigan Ave., Benzonia
231-882-5801
visitbenzie.com

TIP
Register at the visitors bureau and pick up your passport and special "jewel" that in the past year has netted such bonus gifts as a twenty-five-dollar gas card, kite, or water bottle.

BIKE A TART TRAIL

If you need to burn off some of those foodie indulgences or just want to meander over streams and past orchards on a trail easy enough for beginners, the nonprofit Traverse Area Recreation Trails (TART) has options for you amid more than one hundred miles of trails in Grand Traverse and Leelanau Counties. The Leelanau Trail, a scenic favorite, is a seventeen-mile path through forests, meadows, and vineyards, from Traverse City to Suttons Bay. Stroll through the shops and galleries in this quaint village, or grab lunch or a craft brew before pedaling back to TC. If seventeen miles is plenty for you, use the Bay Area Transportation Authority's Bike-n-Ride program to ride back in comfort for three dollars.

OTHER GREAT TART RIDES

Pick up the TART trail behind Brick Wheels and pedal eight miles to Bunker Hill Road in Acme.

The Sleeping Bear Heritage Trail is a twenty-mile trail connecting some of Leelanau County's best attractions.

Mountain bike aficionados will want to check out the Vasa Singletrack Mountain Bike Trail.

Traverse Area Recreational Trails (TART)
P.O. Box 252, Traverse City, MI 49685
231-941-4300
www.traversetrails.org

KAYAK AND BIKE
TO YOUR BREWS

Thank young entrepreneur Troy Daily, who saw how many microbreweries were conveniently situated near the banks of the Boardman River and who liked water recreation so much that he thought he'd combine the two. His original "Paddle for Pints" events still sell out so quickly that that Kayak, Bike & Brew now has its own Warehouse District storefront complete with a post-ride photo booth wall, and many trips are offered daily. Check in for your handy dry bag backpack with sunglasses, get your bike, and explore neighborhoods en route to the first stop and optional wood-fired pizza at The Filling Station; then paddle a kayak across Boardman Lake and likely past a great blue heron or two to Right Brain Brewery, where the "culinary beer" focus might have you sampling a whole cherry pie in a glass—and loving it—before heading on to more.

Kayak, Bike & Brew
229 Garland St., Traverse City
231-760-8828
kayakbikebrew.com

TACKLE A "BEAR"
OF A COURSE

Look on the bright side. The ponds and moguls, bunkers and roughs will muffle your frustration screams, plus you'll have true bragging rights once you tackle The Bear, a legendary Jack Nicklaus design. Like many Northern Michigan courses, this Grand Traverse Resort and Spa course is swimming in accolades, but with play stretching over a massive seven thousand yards, honors include America's top 20 "toughest." It's also gorgeous. No two holes are alike, and Scottish-terraced fairways play up the natural hills and orchards that grace the North.

Not up for the challenge yet? The resort boasts two other courses, and its Grand Traverse Golf Academy lets you learn year-round on heated indoor-outdoor hitting bays; pros also use fun, fun motion-capture technology to analyze your swing side by side with those of the pro circuit greats.

100 Grand Traverse Village Blvd., Acme
231-534-6000
grandtraverseresort.com

TIP
Make your nineteenth-hole dinner reservations at sixteenth-floor Aerie, where high-end dining meets one of the area's best sunset-over-water views.

SUNSET, BONFIRE, AND STARGAZING
AT EMPIRE BEACH

When the sun sinks over the horizon, the evening beach show is just beginning along the Lake Michigan shore, especially within the Sleeping Bear Dunes National Lakeshore. Bonfires are allowed at park beaches, and some, such as Empire Beach, make it easy with parking lots close to the six bonfire pits waiting on the beach. Load your blanket cooler and firewood onto a plastic sled, or bring friends and divvy up the toting; commune with nature and each other as the sky morphs into dramatic shades of pink and purple, clouds become art, air cools, and stars come out. If you're lucky, you can catch the Northern Lights shooting above your shoreline flames.

nps.gov/slbe/index.htm

TIP

Firewood bundles are available on self-serve roadside stands on M-72 between Traverse City and Empire or on M-22. Beach fires are permitted on all mainland Lake Michigan beaches in the National Lakeshore between the water's edge and the first dune. Do not, however, build fires on or near vegetation, and be sure to extinguish carefully with water and clean up all debris before leaving.

WATCH
THE ARABIANS LEAP

For seven weeks in July and August, Olympic-caliber equestrians display the ultimate in horsemanship etiquette as they gather on the edge of Traverse City to perform in garb the Queen would approve of on horses with glistening coats and neatly braided tails. Classes of jumpers and hunters perform simultaneously on several rings in nonstop action with the backdrop of a glistening Grand Traverse Bay. Mixed in are entertainers, such as the canine winners of *America's Got Talent*.

Organizers who transform an empty field into a dressage stadium by constructing thousands of stalls from scratch also help out novice visitors by adding term glossaries to event websites. Or just watch and cheer as horses and riders hurdle up to sixteen jumps in around sixty seconds.

Great Lakes Equestrian Festival
Flintfields Horse Park
6535 Bates Rd., Williamsburg
greatlakesequestrianfestival.com

Hop on Ranch Rudolf

Take a one- or two-hour guided trail ride through the Pere Marquette State Forest and along the Boardman River; campsites and lodge rooms are available on-site.

6841 Brown Ridge Rd., Traverse City
231-947-9529
ranchrudolf.com

Outrider Horseback Riding

Tours are private here, and one-hour, full day, and overnight horse camp options are available.

7922 Ole White Dr., Lake Ann
231-275-7065
outriderhorsebackriding.com

Preserve Historic Sleeping Bear

You'll hop in the wagon and let the horses pull on narrated tours of the Port Oneida Rural Historic District the way the original occupants traveled. Bonnet optional.

3164 W Harbor Hwy. (M-22), Maple City
231-334-6103
phsb.org/horse-and-wagon-tours

HIKE
TO AN OVERLOOK

If the best hikes offer a reward, you can't do better than the sun-dappled waters of Lake Michigan, stretching out forever two hundred feet below, which is what you'll find along the 1.5-mile loop trail at Clay Cliffs Natural Area. The trail meanders uphill through a mature hardwood forest abundant with wildflowers. Blue sky peeks from behind trees on the ridgeline, hinting at the view that awaits during a steady climb along switchbacks.

At the top of the Manitou Overlook (so called for the views of North and South Manitou Islands), you may catch the eagle's nest to the left of the viewing platform or its occupants soaring over the lake as you listen to the roaring surf. Heading back is rewarding, too, as the trail descends into and through a windswept meadow perched above Lake Leelanau.

4755 N Manitou Trl., Lake Leelanau
leelanauconservancy.org

MORE HIKES TO A VIEW

Whaleback Natural Area

About 1.5 miles south of Leland off M-22 is a steeper climb to a similar three-hundred-foot bluff overlook. The trail is one mile long with a flat three-quarter-mile loop at the top of the hill.

1679 N Manitou Trl., Leland

Grand Traverse Commons Natural Area

For a majestic sunrise or moonrise view overlooking Traverse City, hike to the top of the Grand Traverse Commons Natural Area, and take in the view from the bench near the intersection of the Copper Ridge Trail and the Old Orchard Trail. Find the trailhead off Red Drive in Traverse City.

8030 Cottageview Dr., Traverse City

Sleeping Bear Dunes National Lakeshore

The Sleeping Bear Dunes National Lakeshore also offers many opportunities for hiking ending in bluff overlooks of Lake Michigan.

Pyramid Point Trail and
Basch Road, Maple City

TAKE
AN M-22 COLOR TOUR

It beat out such fall foliage favorites as the Blue Ridge Parkway, New Hampshire, and Vermont to be named the nation's best autumn drive. That's reason enough to drive M-22 from Traverse City up the Leelanau Peninsula and down the Lake Michigan shoreline toward Manistee, Arcadia, and Onekama. Quaint towns, wide and sandy beaches, great picnic and dining fare, and stunning overlooks are other reasons for taking this drive. Starting in Traverse City, you hug the bay for most of the drive to Omena, where the road curves inland toward Northport. As you head south past Leland, have your camera ready for the tunnel of trees north of Glen Arbor or the gasp-worthy lake glimpses that just . . . appear. Locals love Weisen's farm stand (one mile off M-22 east of Empire on M-72) for a car snack of sweet/tart Honeycrisp apples.

For route maps and adventure ideas:
m22colortour.com
m22.com/blogs/adventure-starts-here

TIP
Make your way to Arcadia, where a climbing platform marks Inspiration Point and telescopes help you catch a glimpse of the Wisconsin shoreline on a clear day and stunning fall color along the shoreline any day.

FLOAT A RIVER

The Boardman, the Platte, the Manistee, the Crystal. There's no shortage of crystal-clear streams for paddling or a float, but it's such a rite of passage to make the easy float from Riverside Canoe Trips in Honor to Lake Michigan on the Lower Platte River that you'll want to head out before 9:00 a.m. or in the late afternoon to avoid crowds and see the most wildlife. Stock up on picnic supplies at Riverside. En route, keep an eye out for beaver, deer, muskrats, bald eagles, or great blue heron. Leave time to play near the end; as you approach the spot where the river empties into shimmering Lake Michigan, the forest gives way to a rushing current great for swimming, sand banks, dune grass, and blue sky.

Riverside Canoe
5042 N Scenic Hwy., Honor
231-325-5622
canoemichigan.com

TIP

Time your float around the fall salmon run, if you're brave. From mid-September to late October, fish of up to five feet long and thirty pounds zip by here and in the shallow Crystal River like swimming bullets, and it's oh so cool.

TAKE
AMERICA'S PRETTIEST
SEVEN-MILE ROAD TRIP

Think ultimate road trip design and you might sketch in a pretty tree canopy, soft sand for hiking, and some Instagram-worthy pull-offs, or example, a towering dune that falls 450 feet straight into a still blue sea. Michigan lumberman Pierce Stocking kept track of Kodak moments as he worked within the Sleeping Bear Dunes National Lakeshore, and those became the 7.4-mile Pierce Stocking Scenic Drive. He did good. *Good Morning America* viewers once named this the Most Beautiful Place in America based on footage gathered along the drive.

Pierce Stocking Scenic Drive
8500 Stocking Dr., Empire
nps.gov/slbe

TIP
Don't miss the Key West-style sunset moment. Sink into the amphitheater of sand at stop nine for the sinking of the sun, and join the applause. Just don't linger long. The drive closes thirty minutes after sunset.

RUN
THROUGH THE VINEYARDS

One of the most original finish lines in the country is likely the Harvest Stompede's. It's a grape-filled hole in which runners and walkers jump to literally stomp grapes after running through vineyards filled with them. Clearly a one-of-a-kind event, the Stompede includes a 5K walk, a 5K run, or a seven-mile run that offers fun for serious athletes and those liking the idea of a vineyard stroll through rolling hills with stunning bay and vineyard views.

After the race, participants take a self-guided, two-day wine-tasting tour along the Leelanau Peninsula Wine Trail, where food and wine pairings are offered at each winery, and fees are included in the race ticket price.

Leelanau Peninsula Wine Trail
10781 E Cherry Bend Rd., Studio 1, Traverse City
231-642-5550
lpwines.com

GO DOWNHILL SKIING

With five months of winter weather, rolling hills, and an average snowfall of more than a hundred inches, Northern Michigan lends itself to downhill skiing—some of the best in the Midwest. Skiing pioneer Everett Kircher brought the first chairlift ever constructed from Sun Valley, Idaho, when he opened Boyne Mountain in 1948. With the longest runs in Michigan, Boyne is the choice of many serious skiers. For après-ski action, take the chairlift to the Eagle's Nest and have a drink while watching the sun set over the Boyne Valley. If you prefer, the Snowflake Lounge offers live music for your après-ski groove and an outdoor deck, where you can sip a brandy while watching the last skiers glide down the mountain . . . and it's far from the area's only option.

Crystal Mountain Resort

Often ranked best for families, it's celebrating more than sixty years.

12500 Crystal Mountain Dr., Thompsonville
231-668-6628
crystalmountain.com

Boyne Mountain Resort

1 Boyne Mountain Rd., Boyne Falls
855-688-7024
boyne.com

Shanty Creek Resort

Score some great deals here, and visit four terrain parks with five quad chairlifts and two mountains for one lift ticket.

5780 Shanty Creek Rd., Bellaire
shantycreek.com

Hickory Hills

City owned, there's a warming house for sipping hot chocolate around a giant fireplace.

2000 Randolph St., Traverse City
231-947-8566
traversecitymi.gov/hickory_hills.asp

Mount Holiday

A nonprofit with a strong sense of community, it also has a bar for a hot toddy warmup.

3100 Holiday Rd., Traverse City
231-928-2500
mt-holiday.com

SKI
THE VASA

There is one thing you can be sure of in Northern Michigan winters: snow. And lots of it! There's a saying here that there's no such thing as bad weather—just the wrong clothing. Locals and visitors in the know have well-honed skills (and built trails) for enjoying the soft powder that winter brings. The Vasa Pathway is Michigan's premier cross-country ski trail. It features more than twenty-five kilometers that meander along the towering pines and babbling creeks of the Pere Marquette State Forest. There is nothing like (kicking and) gliding through the powder in the crisp Northern Michigan air under a canopy of snow-laden trees. Need to rent equipment? Stop by Brick Wheels or Don Orr Ski Haus. Need instruction? Check out the Weski Program hosted by the Vasa Ski Club, offering one hour of instruction and a light meal for three Sundays in January.

TIP
Ready for the ultimate test? The North American VASA (vasa.org) and its series of classic, freestyle, and fatbike races is the third-largest event of its kind in the United States, typically drawing nearly a thousand skiers.

GET OUT AND ENJOY WINTER

Vasa Pathway

4450 Bartlett Rd., Williamsburg
231-941-4300
traversetrails.org/trail/vasa-pathway

Lost Lake Pathway

6.5-mile, mostly flat, dog-friendly loop near Interlochen
Wildwood Rd., Interlochen
231-922-5280
michigantrailmaps.com/member-profile/3/157

Leelanau State Park

The five-mile Lake Michigan-to-Mud Lake Loop is a
challenge but followed by a rewarding vista.

15310 N Lighthouse Point Rd., Northport
231-386-5422
michigantrailmaps.com/member-profile/3/137

Boardman Valley Trail

Scenic and flat, the 1.5-mile trail hugs the Boardman and
is perfect for beginners.

3000 Racquet Club Dr., Traverse City
231-941-0960
garfield-twp.com/twpnaturereserve.asp

SOAR
LIKE AN EAGLE

The landing strip of a tiny, small-town airport is a surprising place to find one of the most memorable experiences of Michigan's North—or that you might find almost anywhere. That's at least true if you love the scenery of Great Lakes shorelines and forests and from the vantage point of one of the eagles you just may see flying near you.

The Northwest Soaring Club is a group of licensed pilots that likes to introduce others to the beauty (and silence) of glider flight. Don't worry. They'll be along for your ride as another plane—with engine—hauls you high enough to catch the thermals and soar back down for several minutes or much longer, depending on which flight you book. A three-thousand-foot glide runs seventy-five dollars, and you can go higher for a nominal fee.

Northwest Soaring Club
576 Airport Rd., Frankfort
616-352-9160
frankfortdowfield.com/glidinfo.htm

TIP
The scenery is spectacular in fall, when the land
is a quilt-style patchwork of color and Lake Michigan
still a vibrant blue.

SPREAD OUT
AT THE OPEN SPACE

During logging days, it was the city's front door, the center of commerce, where the Boardman River met the bay. Logs were floated from river to bay, and locals bought anything they needed at Perry Hannah's dry goods shop. Today, it's more the front yard for play. The literally named "Open Space" allows for a long view of the bay for anyone driving past and room to roam, walk dogs, bike, fly kites, and spread blankets for everyone else. Soak in the grassy space and sidewalk that edges the bay, and then meander past the city marina and quacking ducks toward Clinch Park's beach party vibe. Have a snack bar treat, let the children play in the water, rent a paddleboard, and plop on the region's most lively stretch of sandy beach, and you've absorbed the essence of this place.

Intersection of Union Street and
W Grandview Parkway, Traverse City

LEARN TO CURL

When winter morphs our area's water wealth to ice, Michiganders still go out to play. Some fish on it, others now go curling—an outing that's especially fun when your learn-to-curl session fee (ten dollars) comes with a five dollar craft beer token at adjacent Stormcloud Brewery. A favorite gathering spot all year, Stormcloud takes on a special aura midwinter when you can sip a Scottish ale and feel like a medieval Scot at the same time, given that they invented the game involving a broom and stone slid down an ice sheet. Stick around and join a league, pick up the fine points for future play, or just sit back and watch with a pint and some truffle-Parmesan-topped popcorn, a flatbread pizza, or an ice cream float made with a porter or a stout.

Stormcloud Brewing Company
303 Main St., Frankfort
231-352-0118
stormcloudbrewing.com

RACE
THE BAYSHORE

There might be a hundred ways the Bayshore Marathon, ways the Bayshore Marathon might hasten one's demise, at least without proper training, but there are more reasons it stands out as king among the region's many and still-growing number of athletic competitions. More than six thousand runners take part in the full marathon, half marathon, and 10K races that all run along the Grand Traverse Bay shoreline for most of the route. Some participate, while many more cheer on the participants during this Memorial Day weekend summer kickoff event, rattling cowbells or spraying the willing and sweaty with garden hoses. Rivaling for best race scenery is the M-22 challenge—a run, bike, and paddle event that begins with a dune climb at the Sleeping Bear Dunes National Lakeshore and includes biking sections along the Crystal River and a paddle in Glen Lake.

Bayshore Marathon
bayshoremarathon.org

M-22 Challenge
m22.com

HANG ZEN

Those who like to mix fitness with pleasure and also spend as much time as they can on the water head out for their yoga on a stand-up paddleboard in the middle of Lake Michigan. At sunset. No, the boards aren't anchored. If you lose your balance, you just fall over into the water and climb back on. When you get the hang of it, you'll have bragging rights aplenty, not to mention frame-worthy proof.

Instructor Anna Mallien will take a photo of your favorite poses on the board—your silhouette on the water, with the orange sky as a backdrop. Mallien offers her yoga on the water classes on Wednesdays at 8:00 p.m. in Empire, or book a private or group class on Lake Michigan, Crystal Lake, or Grand Traverse Bay.

Anna Mallien
Frankfort
231-383-1885
annamallien.com

STRIKE A POSE

In a vineyard
Yen Yoga's Yoga in the Vines
231-421-5496
yenyogafitness.com

On a rooftop at sunrise
Hotel Indigo Traverse City
263 W Grandview Pkwy.
231-932-0500
ihg.com

On a goat farm
Idyll Farms (special occasion)
10901 E Peterson Park Rd., Northport
231-386-7823
idyllfarms.com

On a ski hill
Crystal Mountain Resort
12500 Crystal Mountain Dr., Thompsonville
231-668-6628
crystalmountain.com

SURF
A GREAT LAKE

If Great Lakes surfers have a reputation for insanity, know that's because the best waves kick up around November, when the water is not exactly temperate. Enter the wetsuit—and, yes, a bit of fearlessness. When strong south to southwest winds clamor against the breakwall in Frankfort, you'll find throngs of surfers and kiteboarders to watch as entertainment as they ride the swirling waves that break onshore. Experienced kiteboarders can fly twenty to thirty feet in the air and land fifty feet from where they started.

Even novices can at least give it a spin (hopefully, not literally), with a class from Sleeping Bear Surf & Kayak, which offers stand-up paddleboarding on Lake Michigan or a small inland lake nearby for the just slightly less adventurous.

Sleeping Bear Surf & Kayak
10228 W Front St., Empire
231-326-9283
sbsurfandkayak.com

CHEER
THE BEACH BUMS

You'll cheer for both the Suntan and Sunburn, at least at the Beach Bums, where the huggable characters make for colorful mascots of Traverse City's minor league baseball team. Baseball fans love following the season as the team plays competitors in the East Division of the Frontier League. Almost everybody loves the chance to catch the rocketing T-shirts or watch the mascots' antics while sipping local craft beer, wine, and snacks. When it moved from Indiana in 1995, the franchise became Traverse City's first pro baseball team since 1915.

Crave more organized sports? The Detroit Red Wings hold their September training camp at Traverse City's Centre Ice Arena, and tickets are publicly available for training games.

Traverse City Beach Bums
333 Stadium Dr., Traverse City
traversecitybeachbums.com

Centre Ice Arena
1600 Chartwell Dr., Traverse City
centreice.org

PONDER THE MILKY WAY

Night sky tourism will only get more important as city lights literally erase the ancient constellations and sights of the Milky Way that connect us to past civilizations and the mysteries of what lies beyond.

In both sky preserve and in Michigan's long tracts of undeveloped forests and beaches, you'll see the Milky Way in the southern sky, rising as the night progresses. Or practice your constellation identifications, wish upon a falling star, or ponder the mysteries of the universe in one of these best spots for dialing the world above into focus.

Among the best in the world, the Headlands International Dark Sky Park was established in nearby Emmet County—only the sixth dark sky park in the nation. In TC, Northwestern Michigan College's Rogers Observatory hosts public viewing nights. For a nautical twist, take in the cosmos from an 1800s replica tall ship on the *Manitou*'s astronomy cruise. In Leelanau County, the Sleeping Bear Dunes National Lakeshore hosts stargazing parties in summer. For that matter, spread your blanket on almost any beach in the National Lakeshore. On a clear dark night, you are guaranteed to see the Milky Way emerge while being serenaded by the water lapping gently onshore, or watch for the aurora borealis in the northern sky!

Headlands International Dark Sky Park

15675 Headlands Rd., Mackinaw City
231-436-4015
midarkskypark.org

Joseph H. Rogers Observatory

1753 Birmley Rd., Traverse City
231-946-1787
Information line: 231-995-2300
nmc.edu/resources/observatory/public-viewing.html

Traverse Tall Ship Company

13258 S West Bay Shore Dr., Traverse City
231-941-2000
tallshipsailing.com/specialty-cruises-events

Sleeping Bear Dunes Night Sky Programs

9922 Front St., Empire
231-326-4700, ext. 5005
nps.gov/slbe/planyourvisit/explore-the-night-sky.htm

SNAG
A SALMON

Home to ten blue-ribbon trout streams and more than sixty inland lakes, the Traverse City area is a fisherman's paradise. In spring, steelhead, bass, and trout fill the cold northern waters. In late summer and fall, salmon make their annual trip through Lake Michigan and Grand Traverse Bay into rivers upstream. In winter, shanties and tip-ups pop up on inland lakes for the Northern Michigan tradition of ice fishing. Orvis Streamside sells fly-fishing equipment and offers lessons and guided trips. If you want to get out on the big water, try Big Kahuna Charters. For ice fishing fun, contact Sport Fish Michigan. Or just drop a line into the Boardman River in downtown TC. So, what are you waiting for? Cast away!

Orvis Streamside
223 E Front St., Traverse City
231-933-9300
streamsideorvis.com

Big Kahuna Charters
6455 S West Bay Shore Dr., Traverse City
231-946-7454
bigkahunacharter.com

Sport Fish Michigan
Captain Ben Wolfe
4819 Arbutus Ln., Beulah
231-683-1212
sportfishmichigan.com/ice-fishing

SNORKEL
A SHIPWRECK

In Traverse City's heyday, Lake Michigan and the Grand Traverse Bay carried vessels bound for Chicago and Cleveland, laden with Northern Michigan lumber and iron ore, but those caught in the lakes' frequent storms remain on the bottom, sometimes accessible from shore.

Snorkelers can explore the eerie remains of the *Metropolis*, a 126-foot wooden schooner that sank just off Old Mission Peninsula in 1886, or the *Rising Sun*, a 133-foot wooden steamer resting in just six feet of water near Pyramid Point. Besides shipwrecks, several shore dives are steeped in local history. The "junk pile," including an intact Ford Pinto, is attributed to teenage mischief in the 1950s. Scuba North provides equipment and maps, letting you take a guided tour, or grab some flippers and set off on your own.

Scuba North
833 S Garfield Ave., Traverse City
231-947-2520
scubanorth.com

RIDE A FATBIKE
ON A SNOWY TRAIL

Traverse City takes its cycling seriously, and when winter blows into town, the adventurous—and curious—roll out (or rent) the fatties—bikes designed with oversized tires that glide through sand or snow with ease. Check out the Vasa Pathway trail map for groomed fatbike trails for beginners (3K Meadows Loop) or those ready to throw down (15K singletrack). Rent a fatbike at Brick Wheels or McClain Cycle. If you go to Crystal Mountain in Thompsonville or Timber Ridge Resort in Traverse City, you can find lit groomed trails and fatbike rentals on-site. Both let you cozy up next to the massive fireplace with some hot chocolate after your ride and jaw about who was gnarliest on the trail (while the icicles on your eyelashes thaw out).

Vasa Pathway

4450 Bartlett Rd., Williamsburg
231-941-4300
traversetrails.org/fatbike-trails

Brick Wheels

736 E Eighth St., Traverse City
231-947-4274
brickwheels.com

McClain Cycle and Fitness

750 E Eighth St., Traverse City
231-941-7161
mclaincycle.com

Timber Ridge RV and Recreation Resort

4050 Hammond Rd. E, Traverse City
231-947-2770
timberridgeresort.net

Crystal Mountain Resort

12500 Crystal Mountain Dr., Thompsonville
231-668-6628
crystalmountain.com

HUNT (FOR ROCKS)

Beachcombing counts as the best entertainment in these parts, suitable as the center even of a day's gathering with friends, and when not just looking for the perfectly smooth flat rock to skip, "hunters" with that trademark stoop are generally looking for two particular stones. Petoskey stones are remnants of a massive colony of coral from awhile back (350 million years ago). Petrified over millennia and dislodged by glaciers, they are covered with beautiful hexagons that flaunt their prehistoric heritage, especially perfect when wet or polished, and found from Empire north on the Lake Michigan shoreline. Stick close to Leland for the "Leland Blue" formed from the heaps of slag dumped into the harbor by the iron industry in the late 1800s. A by-product of smelting iron ore, they've become revered for their sea-blue color.

Hall Beach (aka Van's Beach)
205 Cedar St., Leland
leelanauconservancy.org/blog/naturalarea/hall-beach

Petoskey State Park
2475 M-119, Petoskey
231-347-2311
dnr.state.mi.us/parksandtrails

LEARN THAT LIFE
REALLY IS A BEACH

You might title this book "All I really needed to know I learned at the beach"—undeniably the best spot for meditation, time with friends, play. The famed "Dr. Beach" has ranked the joint beaches of the Sleeping Bear Dunes National Lakeshore number one in the Midwest, but that's pretty obvious anyway as you stroll uncrowded swaths of sand edged by cliffs of sometimes hardwoods and sometimes massive dunes of sand, jump the waves, skip some stones, and (in season) explore dramatic ice caves. For the best secret in town, head to Maple Bay Natural Area, south of Elk Rapids on East Grand Traverse Bay. See and be seen (and get access to snack bars and chair rentals) at Clinch Park Beach right downtown, and for the best sunrise, head to East Bay Park Beach, and so begins another day in paradise.

traversecity.com/summer/outdoors/beaches

CULTURE AND HISTORY

EMBRACE
YOUR INNER FUDGIE

For fifty years, Doug Murdick's Fudge in Traverse City has been crafting decadence through molten chocolate turned on cool slabs for every visitor to see—and, craftily, to smell. The result has been so many boxes of fudge sold that tourists in the northern part of Michigan have been given the moniker "fudgie." Some say the term came from 1887 when a Mackinac Island candymaker peddled "I'm a fudgie" buttons. Whatever the root, it's a bit of a rule that you're not on vacation until you've at least sampled fudge or caramel corn or seasonal caramel apples.

The original Murdick's actually opened on Mackinac Island in 1887, the same year as the Grand Hotel, and the popularity spread to franchises on Front Street and U.S. 31 (marked with a giant box of fudge on the roof).

Doug Murdick's Fudge
116 E Front St., Traverse City
231-947-4841

Murdick's Fudge
4500 U.S. 31 North, Traverse City
231-938-2330
murdicksfudge.com
209 N St. Joseph St., Suttons Bay
231-271-4445
murdicksfudgeshoppe.com

SLEEP
LIKE IT'S 1910

"It's kind of a happy time in our American history. There was not a lot of political strife, and it was kind of quiet on the home front. And it's quiet out here. Like a little bubble." That's how Susan Odom, who wears vintage dresses like the "summer sheer frock" of the era, describes a stay to guests at her Hillside Homestead farm bed and breakfast. Oil lamps illuminate the vintage dining table, music emanates from the pump organ in the parlor, and even her made-in-house maple-cured bacon is cooked on the massive wood stove. History is also shared as exciting dinner table conversation, whether it's lard's bad rap or how a Hoosier cabinet was sold to save women steps. But the best entertainment? Sitting in the porch swing under a brilliant night sky.

Hillside Homestead
3400 N Setterbo Rd., Suttons Bay
231-271-1131
hillsidehomestead.com

TIP
You don't have to be an overnight guest to book one of Odom's historic dinners, for which recipes are drawn from her collection of eight hundred period cookbooks.

CAMP
LIKE A POP STAR

The likes of *Breaking Bad*'s Vince Gilligan, actress Felicity Huffman, and such singers as Norah Jones, Josh Groban, and Jewell once trotted around Interlochen Arts Academy as students or art school campers. A new series of classes for adults now lets all wannabe actors, painters, and writers or those seeking to add a little creativity to their lives be similarly inspired by the woodsy, lakefront campus near Traverse City.

Small group classes might run a few hours or maybe a full week, featuring such topics as watercolor journaling, Shakespearean acting, mystery writing, fiber dying, and even playing the ukelele. For a bonus, attend a concert or play, or just soak in the music wafting from student practice rooms.

Interlochen Center for the Arts
4000 S M-137 Hwy., Interlochen
interlochen.org

TIP
Fully immerse yourself by eating in the student cafeteria and staying in an on-campus cottage; some come with their own beachfront.

HELP LIGHT THE WAY

Michigan has more lighthouses (120) than any other state, and while diehard fans look to mark each "spotting" off a life list, those interested can also "keep" one as a volunteer lighthouse keeper for a weekend or a week at two lighthouses near Traverse City.

Neither the circa-1920s Grand Traverse Lighthouse Museum near Northport nor the Old Mission Lighthouse at the tip of Old Mission Peninsula still acts as a navigational aid, but they're still key tourist and educational draws. You won't learn more than you will by acting as a volunteer (for a small fee) staffing the gift shop, keeping up the journal and grounds, and living by the pounding waves as keepers once did.

Point Betsie in nearby Frankfort lets guests stay too, but it runs as a more traditional B&B in which you can vacation for two nights up to a week.

traversecity.com/things-to-do/attractions/lighthouses

WANDER FISHTOWN

Make your way to Leland, where a left-hand turn off Main Street toward the marina takes you to the historic commercial fishing village of Fishtown, where the Leland River separates Lake Leelanau and Lake Michigan. Book a charter or sunset cruise, or just walk along the docks past weathered fishing shanties, smokehouses, and racks of drying fishing nets. Leave time to wander, too, among the shanties that have been converted to visit-worthy boutiques of gifts, clothing, and galleries.

Go ahead and snap a picture (many thousands before you have) of historic river tugs, such as the *Janice Sue* and *Joy*, with Lake Michigan in the distance. You can also learn Fishtown history on a series of historic markers. It was listed on the National Register of Historic Places in 1975.

Leland
231-256-8878
fishtownmi.org

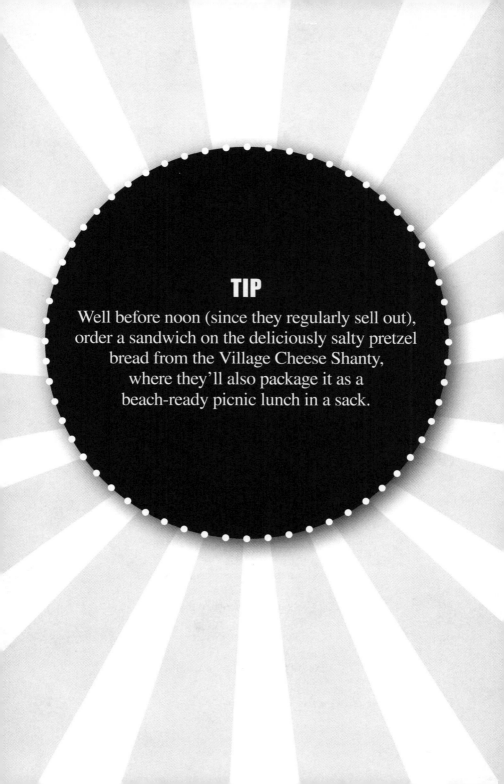

TIP

Well before noon (since they regularly sell out), order a sandwich on the deliciously salty pretzel bread from the Village Cheese Shanty, where they'll also package it as a beach-ready picnic lunch in a sack.

START
A COTTAGE TRADITION

Cultural anthropologist Brian Hoey once centered a lifestyle migration study around the Traverse City area, fascinated by the way so many people migrated to permanent living after being introduced to the region through multigenerational cottage stays. Enjoy Michigan "slow travel" cottage traditions, in other words, and you'll likely be hooked. That's especially true at such old-time but upscale resorts as Watervale (circa 1917, Arcadia), Chimney Corners (circa 1910, Frankfort), and Fountain Point (circa 1889, Lake Leelanau), where in some cases guests once arrived by steamboat and buggy, and today's common threads include breezy porches, board games, family reconnection, and communal dining with new friends. The Wednesday evening picnic and Friday-night Lodge Dinners at Chimney Corners are so popular that the resort has published its own cookbook with the recipes.

Watervale Inn
244 Watervale Rd., Arcadia
231-352-9083, watervaleinn.com

Chimney Corners Resort
1602 Crystal Dr., Frankfort
231-352-7522, chimneycornersresort.com

Fountain Point Resort
990 S Lake Leelanau Dr., Lake Leelanau
231-256-9800, fountainpointresort.com

TIME TRAVEL
ON A MAGICAL HISTORY TOUR

The fun of a tour with a guide armed with a set of old photographs of Traverse City is the chance to jump around in time without the jet lag. Once a week from mid-June through mid-October, a docent affiliated with the Traverse Area Historical Society waits in front of Horizon Books to lead a storytelling session that takes you back.

You'll learn how Horizon Books became the downtown anchor that helped fuel a Front Street renaissance, and your guide might recall childhood memories of films at the Lyric Theatre before it was renovated to become the State Theatre. While you might head today to buy a cool bag at Votruba Leather Goods, it was founded to make saddles for horses. While stopping in front of what's now an upscale French bistro but used to be a fire station, you may even see a snapshot of two of the city's most famous working horses, those that used to pull the fire truck.

Traverse Area Historical Society
Downtown Walking and Cemetery Tours
231-995-0313
traversehistory.wordpress.com

CHANNEL
THE SILK STOCKING SET

You can meet Perry Hannah, Traverse City's founder, in a few ways on a downtown stroll, starting with his statue at 6th and Cass, where he may be holding a pine cone today or sporting a jaunty hat or shades tomorrow. Those who've researched the founding father say he wouldn't mind at all; his plan was for a town that would bring people of all walks together, and he wouldn't likely want to be missing out. Stroll 6th Street to see his onetime home, a four-story mansion that's now the Reynolds-Jonkhoff Funeral Home, and also note the way all the 6th Street porches line up, something he supposedly insisted on in his well-planned town. In the late 1890s, this was dubbed "Silk Stocking Row" for the way lumber and manufacturing barons could afford to live there.

TIP

Stay at the Park Place Hotel, which was once the Hannah-built Campbell House, both for its historic features and for the way you can see the whole city he plotted from the upper floor (and very fun) lounge; note how the churches are clustered. He donated land to every denomination.

Park Place Hotel
300 E State St., Traverse City
231-946-5000
park-place-hotel.com

TAKE THE TUNNEL TOUR

Head with a guide behind sometimes boarded-up doors and into underground steam tunnels of a onetime state mental hospital. It's a compelling way to learn how the philosophy "beauty is therapy" was integrated into one of the nation's most unusual and successful adaptive development projects—and one likely to prompt a shiver or two.

The progressive mid- to late-nineteenth-century Kirkbride mental health model posited that "beauty is therapy," which is an idea that applies today to the grounds where a village of buttery yellow brick buildings topped with castle-style turrets house high-end restaurants, boutiques, and tasting rooms surrounded by hiking trails. Guided Historic Walking Tours head into yet-to-be-developed areas, where signs point out such features as the "Women's Most Disturbed Ward" and both walls (graffiti) and guides share poignant tales.

The Village at Grand Traverse Commons
1200 W 11th St., Traverse City
231-941-1900
thevillagetc.com

TIP

Book ahead; tours starting at twenty-five dollars and themed around the tunnels, twilight, and photography all fill up fast in peak summer. Be sure to save time to stick around and use coupons to sample wood-fired Parmesan olive herb bread at a former fire station and Trattoria Stella's farm-to-fork Italian fare made by a James Beard-nominated chef.

LEARN
FROM THE FIRST NATION

The word *eyaawing* translates to "who we are," and at the Eyaawing Museum & Cultural Center, the Grand Traverse Band of Ottawa and Chippewa Indians shares the story of the region's original people through both multimedia displays and gifts. Every guest is invited to take with them a sacred bundle of sweet grass, sage, tobacco, and cedar, handwrapped in fabric scraps and tied with a bow, to be spread with a thankfulness prayer by water or fire or earth. The soaring building with its roof designed with ripples to mimic the waves of adjacent Grand Traverse Bay is located in what was once called "Eagle Town," now called Peshawbestown (as you'll learn) to honor an early chief. The centerpiece of the museum is two eagles in flight, talons locked, poignant since the tribe's prophecy foretold they'd again be a great nation when the eagles (now plentiful) returned.

Eyaawing Museum & Cultural Center
2304 N West Bay Shore Dr., Suttons Bay
231-534-7764
gtbindians.org/eyaawing.asp

HELP SAIL
A TALL SHIP

Captains of the tall ship *Manitou* like to dub their trips "forced relaxation," particularly true on the multiday schooner sails on which the wind dictates the destination. Passengers join in chants and work as they "ready, heave, haul away" and position the three hundred feet of canvas to catch the wind on one of the biggest sailing vessels on the Great Lakes. Longer sails might be themed around the night sky or music or wine, and guests eat food cooked on a woodstove and learn about sailing life of the 1850s basically by living it. Day sails include one featuring ice cream, evening sails catch the bay's fading light, and there's a bed-and-breakfast option for those wanting a lullaby of rocking waves.

Traverse Tall Ship Company
13258 S West Bay Shore Dr., Traverse City
231-941-2000
tallshipsailing.com

LEARN
WHILE YOU DANCE

Every August the Grand Traverse Band of Ottawa Indians offers the public a glimpse into its rich culture at its annual powwow. It's a sacred ceremony—a celebration of tradition, and a reunion, too, of family and friends. The drum circle provides a heartbeat, while high-pitched chanting tells ancient stories in a universal language. "Jingle dancers" in handcrafted regalia form a circle. (Each clash of the dress's jingle cones, made from rolled tobacco lids, represents a prayer to the creator.) You may find yourself in the middle of this whirl of color and sound, when the emcee invites "all nations" to dance. Or you may decide instead to wander among the vendors displaying quillwork or black ash baskets or try a traditional dish, such as tasty fry bread or wild rice soup.

gtbindians.org

OTHER OPPORTUNITIES TO EXPERIENCE A POWWOW

The Grand Traverse Band presents a "powwow dance" each year at heritage day during the National Cherry Festival, held in Traverse City, during the second week in July.

The Grand Traverse Band holds a New Years Eve Sobriety Powwow every year at the Grand Traverse Resort.

The Little River Band of Ottawa Indians, a neighboring tribe, also has an annual powwow, which is generally held the first weekend of July in Manistee.

gtbindians.org
lrboi-nsn.gov

HANG WITH HEMINGWAY

Toss a line into the Boardman River and you might be channeling Ernest Hemingway, who once fished off an area bridge while camping and "traded fish for milk," but it's worth venturing an hour or so north to find the best clues to his life and inspiration. Charlevoix's Museum at Harsha House houses his marriage certificate to first wife Hadley Richardson. Petoskey's Little Traverse History Museum has the typewriter he used while standing up due to "war wounds," and its City Park Grill features the stool upon which he'd often drink. But Horton Bay is where he spent the summers of his youth, and says local expert and tour guide Chris Struble, "I don't know of any small town with five houses and two roads that any artist has ever used as a backdrop more times."

Petoskey Yesterday Hemingway Tours
306 E Lake St. (located inside the Arlington Jewelers store), Petoskey
517-290-3162
petoskeyyesterday.com

TOUR
THE HOBBIT HOMES

Since it's much closer than Middle Earth, it's worth driving about an hour north to Charlevoix for a self-guided tour of the works of architect Earl Young. One of Charlevoix's first architects, Young moved to town in 1900 when it was a rutted dirt road bordered by wood-plank sidewalks and gas lanterns. He became enamored of the boulders he'd find while exploring, prompting a collection and eventual work as an apprentice stonemason. Many of his still-standing designs were part of an early luxury Lake Michigan resort called Boulder Park, and both boulders and whimsy characterize the thirty structures he built in the area. Pick up a map at the Museum at Harsha House and then walk to designs marked by wavy roofs that seem to fly, one sporting a thatched roof imported from England and a "Half House" that seems designed for hobbits or fairies.

Museum at Harsha House
103 State St., Charlevoix
231-547-0373
chxhistory.com

VISIT
A SECRET GARDEN

For more than two decades, Dee Blair has spent her early morning hours in summer creating a magnificent walled garden at her 1894 Queen Anne Victorian home. Visitors may tour it for free if the "open" sign is on the front lawn. Follow the brick path around to the arched rustic door, ring the charming entry bell, and step back in time into a lush secret garden. The sound of water trickling into fountains creates instant tranquility, as visitors follow stone paths through the various garden "rooms." Fairies and gargoyles peek out from between a hundred different plants and flowers. English and Welsh statues guard the ivy and clematis vines trailing down handmade trellises. Sit on one of the benches, breathe in the lavender, and enjoy this feast for the senses.

Sunnybank Gardens
325 Sixth St., Traverse City
231-929-4351
deeblair.com

GET INTO INUIT ART

It would perhaps seem logical that photos of Northern Michigan beachscapes and maybe even a statue of a whitetail deer might greet you at the entrance to the Dennos Museum Center at Traverse City's Northwestern Michigan College—at least more so than a massive polar bear and a musk ox. Enter the Inuit Gallery and peruse the collection of 1,500 tapestries, sculptures, and more from the Canadian Arctic, though, and you'll understand. The polar-themed collection was started in 1960 and has grown to become one of the largest and most complete of its kind. A museum expansion now allows the chance to showcase other exhibits, including Japanese prints, Great Lakes Indian art, and traveling exhibits, and to better host guests, such as Tibetan monks making mandalas or conversations about Great Lakes exploration.

1701 E Front St., Traverse City
231-995-1055
dennosmuseum.org

TIP
Don't miss the gallery that showcases photographic works, including a rare piece by Edward Weston. The museum owns one of four known copies of this image, and another sold at auction for $1.6 million.

EXPLORE
THE HUMAN HISTORY OF THE DUNES

Most often stories of the Sleeping Bear Dunes National Lakeshore focus on the towers of sand that tourists once explored by dune buggy and today climb by foot and run down with broad smiles. Sometimes, the focus is on the Ojibwe tale of how they were formed—how cubs fled a Wisconsin fire with their mom (the big dune) but didn't make it and became the two picturesque Manitou Islands. You'll learn a bit of it all at Glen Haven, where rangers at the U.S. Coast Guard Museum memorably demonstrate the way ships were once saved in the perilous Manitou Passage. Bike in by the Sleeping Bear Heritage Trail, watch the village smithy work his magic, buy penny candy in the restored general store where lumbermen and families once shopped, or just head to sandy Glen Haven beach, which holds plenty of human history of its own.

Historic Glen Haven
Sleeping Bear Dunes National Lakeshore
Glen Haven Rd., Glen Arbor
nps.gov/slbe/planyourvisit/glen-haven-historic-village

FUN FACT

Between 1871 and 1915, crews at the Coast
Guard station in Glen Haven saved 178,000 people
with a success rate of 99 percent. Today, rangers
demonstrate the effective methods with daring
rescues of Raggedy Ann and Andy.

HELP
BLESS THE BLOSSOMS

The first known Blessing of the Blossoms was in 1910, and there's something refreshing about a ritual that's changed little in more than a century. Each year on a May Sunday when fields have bloomed into billowing white and pink clouds, a local pastor presides over a service that integrates natural beauty, readings, and a blessing—of the crops and the fields and those who work them. Today, it's a cap to a weekend wine tour event that highlights first vintages with prerelease barrel tasting and food pairings. The Sunday event honors the region's native heritage with a baptismal sprinkling of holy water in four directions and has a fitting benediction: free cherry pie. A little-known fact is that the ceremony was the precursor to today's National Cherry Festival.

Chateau Chantal
15900 Rue de Vin, Traverse City
231-223-4110
chateauchantal.com

Brengman Brothers Crain Hill Vineyard
9720 S Center Hwy., Traverse City
231-946-2764
brengmanbrothers.com

Grand Traverse Bike Tours
318 N St. Joseph St., Suttons Bay
231-421-6815
suttonsbaybikes.com

TIP

Look for other ways to honor the blossoms, Northern Michigan style, including a Feast of St. Vincent party and vine blessing at Brengman Brothers Crain Hill Winery. Or choose immersion. Suttons Bay-based Grand Traverse Bike Tours offers a fun two-wheeled tasting tour by trail or through the middle of a vineyard.

SHOPPING AND FASHION

SPORT A BAABAAZUZU
ON THE SKI HILL

Fashion and function don't always go together come a cold, snowy winter day, but they do with Baabaazuzu, which adds (soft, fun) fashion and much-needed color to one of Northern Michigan's many snow globe stretches.

The company, located on a rural Leelanau County road, creates eco-fashion by repurposing sweaters into mittens, cloche hats, sweaters, accessories, and bags. Like the greatest inventions, this one was born by an oops—sweaters that shrank in a too-hot dryer. Today, these patchwork-style pieces are one-of-a-kind works of art, sold in galleries around the region and country, and they're often accented by buttons or other fun adornments. As Baabaazuzu shares, "Every piece is an inspired original, just like the person who wears it."

1006 S Sawmill Rd., Lake Leelanau
231-256-7176
baabaazuzu.com

SHOP THE MERCATO

Malls rarely come with buttery yellow brick walls that turn maze-like from one long corridor of shops and restaurants to the next, but then few are Italian-style villages repurposed from a onetime mental hospital topped with castle turrets. Sanctuary Handcrafted Goods, with its often colorful and ethically sourced handicrafts, fits particularly well in the soaring space. Vintage du Jour fittingly offers fun finds from eras past. Boutiques sport fashionable dresses and shirts with Michigan's signature mitten; bookstores are decked with vintage typewriters, first editions, and other fix font size and spacing.

The fun part of a trip, though, is the village feel; you may find an indoor farmers market lining the hallway on any given day, given day, as well as a place a place to do yoga, grab coffee with a friend, or enjoy farm-to-table Italian in a cozy bistro.

The Village at Grand Traverse Commons
830 Cottageview Dr., #101, Traverse City
231-941-1900
thevillagetc.com

FIND
THE TEA YENTA

Visit the headquarters of Light of Day Organics, but before you browse the bright shop stacked floor to ceiling with colorful tea tins, owner Angela Macke may have you sample a matcha tea smoothie she swears is health magic or send you to her lush gardens to walk amid the orange calendula or blue cornflowers. A trained RN, Macke believes the body calls you to what you need. If drawn to those flowers, she may suggest her award-winning Creamy Earl Gray. If the coriander speaks, it might be her Lemony-Ginger Sunshine that you crave, or maybe you'll pick up your message through Happy Green Spleen, the Bun in the Oven blend, or just the ceremony of a cup of tea done right. You'll learn both history and ritual when you enroll in a class held in the garden teepee.

Light of Day Organics
3502 E Traverse Hwy., Traverse City
231-228-7234
lightofdayorganics.com

TIP

Light of Day blends like Sun in the Winter are never as enlightening as when sipped at nearby Crystal Spa, where they're served in a relaxation room by a fireplace or at the outdoor hot tub on the four-season patio.

Crystal Spa
Crystal Mountain
12500 Crystal Mountain Dr., Thompsonville
231-668-6628
crystalmountain.com/crystal-spa/home

SHOP
WHERE FORD AND EDISON DID

General store or theater stage? You'll not be at all sure (and won't at all care) when Old Mission General Store owner Jim Richards, a trained Shakespearean actor and historian, asks to help you in hat and cape, voice booming out true and tall tales across the circa-1850 store with shelves stocked with penny candy, raccoon-skin caps, and high-end cheese and wine. The first retail store between Fort Wayne and Mackinac is in some ways not that different (though far sturdier than the original wigwam) from when a sixteen-year-old founded it with dreams of fur trade–style riches. His penciled notations for snake oil and bittersweet are still on cases. Later, Henry Ford installed Michigan's second gas station here and picked up supplies with friend Thomas Edison. Today, it's where to come for things you never knew you needed—and the fun.

18250 Mission Rd., Traverse City
231-223-4310
oldmissiongeneralstore.com

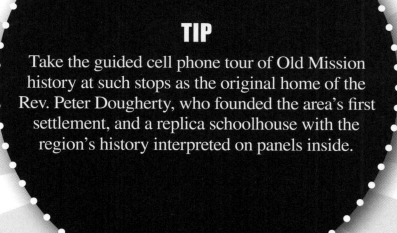

TIP

Take the guided cell phone tour of Old Mission history at such stops as the original home of the Rev. Peter Dougherty, who founded the area's first settlement, and a replica schoolhouse with the region's history interpreted on panels inside.

STOP
AND SMELL THE BLOSSOMS

Stop and smell the irises. Or lavender. Or zinnias. And then pick your own keepsake bouquet—in the case of the clearly named Iris Farm—from among the one-thousand-plus German iris varieties that blanket this picturesque six-acre site five miles from downtown Traverse City. Photographers love the hundreds of neatly lined rows of vivid purple, pink, burgundy, red, orange, and yellow irises that pretty up a cottage table or home garden. On the Old Mission Peninsula, lavender is the star of the new Secret Garden and related gift shop at Brys Estate Vineyard and Winery, and the relaxation-inducing scent wafts across the blooms growing by hilly vineyards as if in Provence. Creativity can run wild when your destination is Omena Cut Flowers, where a self-serve u-pick farm offers a riot of color along Omena Bay.

Iris Farm
5385 E Traverse Hwy., Traverse City
231-947-9040, michigan.org/property/iris-farm

Brys Estate Vineyard and Winery
3309 Blue Water Rd., Traverse City
231-223-9303, brysestate.com

Omena Cut Flowers
12401 E Freeland Rd., Suttons Bay
231-883-8327, omenacutflowers.com

APPLES, SCHMAPPLES!
HEAD TO WHERE CHERRY IS KING

There's no use resisting a store with an in-house cafe and the mantra "Life, Liberty, Beaches and Pie." Inside, there is pie and ice cream too, and some 270 other things made from cherries, be it fruit covered with chocolate or in pulled pork or jam or salsa or coffee or mustard.

TV host Rachael Ray once noted, "If Disney did cherries, the result would look like Cherry Republic." A visit alone makes for a fun ride in this store of whimsical signs and activities, such as a championship cherry pit spit arena. Generous samplings are also available, even of soda and wine—twelve cherry-themed varieties of Boom Chugga Lugga soda for children of all ages, along with Balatan, cherry ciders, and wines for the grown-ups.

Cherry Republic
6026 S Lake St., Glen Arbor
231-226-3014

154 E Front St., Traverse City
231-932-9205

cherryrepublic.com

GET LOST
IN A BOOKSTORE

Traverse City is a town for book lovers. *Publishers Weekly* once made that claim, and you'll agree after taking your own book crawl through shops that each have a distinct personality and rare booksellers who love matching needs to reads. Traverse City's downtown anchor, Horizon Books, is open from 7:00 a.m. to 11:00 p.m. every day, with three floors of books, dozens of magazines, a popular café, and plenty of room to spread out. At Brilliant Books, which has a hang-out worthy vibe and eclectic book selection, many handpicked by owner Peter Makin, you're sure to find (cue British accent) something "Brilliant!" Consider joining the popular, staff-curated book-of-the-month club. The nearby Bookie Joint has great used books for beach reads and funky memorabilia, and lovers of rare and out-of-print books (and vintage typewriters) should leave time for quirky Landmark Books at the Grand Traverse Commons.

Horizon Books
243 E Front St., Traverse City
231-946-7290
horizonbooks.com

Brilliant Books
118 E Front St., Traverse City
231-946-2665
brilliant-books.net

SMALL-TOWN BOOKSTORES MAKE IT WORTH EXTENDING YOUR TOUR

Cottage Book Shop in Glen Arbor, in a log cabin moved intact to the spot and where enclosed porches house best-sellers, regional favorites, and more.

cottagebooks.com

The Bookstore is a fun full-service bookstore with games and gift items too.

facebook.com/frankfortbookstore

Dog Ears Books in Northport is a cozy store attached to an elegant gallery for books used and new and where the bookstore pup will greet you as you might browse an unexpected section on Theodore Roosevelt alongside local favorites and curated finds.

dogearsbooks.net

Have a latte on the charming patio before browsing at **Leelanau Books** in Leland.

leelanaubooks.com

Find George and Merry Ball, who operate **Good Old Books** from their home in Leland out of love of used, old, and rare books.

lelandmi.com/find-a-business/shopping/good-old-books.html

WEAR HOME
YOUR BEACH REMINDER

When we say it's good to wear home a reminder of your beach explorations, we don't mean the piles of soft sand you'll likely be tracking with you. Jewelry crafted from beach stones is the Traverse City equivalent of the Florida souvenir gift made with seashells. Start your search at Korner Gem, which for thirty years has crafted jewelry out of beach finds. If you can't pick between the Petoskey or the Leland Blue, select the popular Unity Bead collection with one on each side. Suttons Bay's Painted Bird and Great Goods are both notable for artsy creations made from beach glass and high-end artistry from natural materials. That's also the hallmark of local artist Becky Thatcher.

Korner Gem
13031 S Fisherman Cove, Traverse City
231-929-9175, kornergem.com

The Painted Bird
216 N St. Joseph St., Suttons Bay
231-271-3050, painted-bird.com

Great Goods
305 N St. Joseph St., Suttons Bay
231-271-0026, great-goods.net

Becky Thatcher Designs
234 E Front St., Traverse City
231-947-5088, beckythatcherdesigns.com

BE UPLIFTED BY ART

When you enter under a colorful awning decked with a fish made of found objects and then are greeted by whimsical, sometimes life-sized sculptures of women in hats made of pears or birds or a crown like the sun (variations of Picasso's *Woman in a Green Hat (Madame Cezanne)* from a recent exhibit), you know you're in for a treat as you always are at Michigan Artists Gallery. The contemporary gallery boasts a wide view of the Boardman River from a deck, its interior design playing off the water, Frank Lloyd Wright style. Nearly 100 percent of the work comes from Michigan artists, and it's often quirky and always fascinating. The shop was named an essential art venue in "100 Best Art Towns in America," and, says owner Sue Ann Round, "Our mission is to create an environment that's very uplifting because there's so much serious in the world."

317 E Front St., Traverse City
231-943-1236, michiganartistsgallery.com

TIP

If you're craving more art, Traverse City and surrounding towns all offer regular art walks and galleries galore, and the waterfront Suttons Bay Art Festival is a must-visit.

SHOP FRONT STREET

Pass the street musicians and fruit trees decked in twinkle lights lining the sidewalks, take the offered sample of fresh-made caramel corn, and head into one of the more than 150 downtown boutiques and galleries mostly centered on Front Street. Shopping and people-watching are hard to separate here, but such specialty clothing shops as Eleven the Shop, Daisy Jane, and What to Wear are worth a close look for more upscale finds. Nest has furniture to glassware, and Cali's and Ella's mix it up with hip fashions and furnishings. Backcountry Outfitters and Boyne Country Sport meet gear and even rental needs as you plan your active fun, and be sure to make a stop at Toy Harbor for everything you'll need for the cabin or the beach. Afterward, hit Mama Lu's for a cucumber habanero margarita and gourmet taco.

Traverse City Area Chamber of Commerce
202 East Grandview Pkwy., Traverse City
231-947-5075
tcchamber.org
downtowntc.com

WEAR A ROAD SIGN
AS A LIFESTYLE STATEMENT

When a couple of entrepreneurial brothers who were experts in kiteboarding started thinking of the drive that connected their favorite boarding spots and activities, they realized the common link was Highway M-22. They put a logo of the sign on a T-shirt, sold them from a van, and later successfully patented the logo. Someone spotted a public photo, and it went viral as symbolic of the dunes, bays, beaches, vineyards, cottages, and nature-drive fun all accessible along that stretch of road. Today at one of their several stores and outlets, you can buy the sign on a T-shirt or sweatshirt, biking shorts, and wine labels as well as postcards with close-ups of a toe making that first dip into water off a dock. As a store mural reads: "It's not just a road. It's a way of life."

M22
125 E Front St., Traverse City
231-360-9090

6298 W Western Ave. (M-22), Glen Arbor
231-334-4425

m22.com

TRY SOME
FEEL-GOOD FASHION

A land blessed by pure, freshwater seas draws people conscious of preserving what nature has gifted, and the bonus is clothing and gifts that both feel good and do good. Yana Dee in downtown Traverse City sells handmade women's and girls' clothing from soy, hemp, bamboo, and salvaged linen. Haystacks (Traverse City, Suttons Bay, Leland, Elk Rapids, and Glen Arbor) is another homegrown company that began with Lizzi Lambert cutting material on her dining room table and has grown with the popularity of her fun prints, swirling hemlines, and practicality for travel. Try on a "switchstack" (a reversible skirt, pants, or top, sometimes made with vintage material). In My Secret Stash, you will find Michigan-made T-shirts, jewelry, accessories, and home décor, many bearing the iconic mitten logo—handy because pointing to the hand is how we show where we live and where we traveled!

Yana Dee Shop
157 E Front St., Traverse City
231-394-0808, yanadee.com

Haystacks
232 E Front St., Traverse City
231-421-3194, haystacks.net

My Secret Stash
122 Cass St., Traverse City
231-929-0340, mysecretstash.com

SUGGESTED
ITINERARIES

CLASSIC TRAVERSE CITY

FROLIC ON FRONT

SPRING FEVER

Fete the Asparagus, 44

Pick morels, 18

Bless the blossoms, 120

ENJOY A WINTER WONDERLAND

Ski the VASA, 78

Ride a fatbike, 92

Go downhill skiing, 76

Drink hot chocolate at Grocer's Daughter, 12

LINGER IN LEELANAU

No soup for you except on Wednesdays, 25

Wander Fishtown, 102

Pierce Stocking Scenic Drive, 74

Explore the history of the dunes, 118

Pleva's, 3

Hop Lot, 43

Visit food artisans, 27

Baabaazuzu, 124

Try a centuries-old apple, 28

MEANDER UP OLD MISSION

Old Mission General Store, 128

Eat with a ghost, 7

Take a selfie on the 45th, 40

Stay at a winery B&B, 57

WORSHIP THE WATER

HAVE FUN WITH THE FAMILY

INDEX